Cain and Abel at Work

ALSO BY GERRY LANGE AND TODD DOMKE

The Conservative's Dictionary

ALSO BY TODD DOMKE

Grounded

CAIN AND ABEL
AT WORK

◆ ◆ ◆

*How to Overcome Office Politics and the
People Who Stand Between You and Success*

◆ ◆ ◆

GERRY LANGE
AND TODD DOMKE

BROADWAY BOOKS
NEW YORK

BROADWAY

Broadway Books titles may be purchased for business or promotional use or for special sales. For information, please write to: Special Markets Department, Random House, Inc., 1540 Broadway, New York, NY 10036.

BROADWAY BOOKS and its logo, a letter B bisected on the diagonal, are trademarks of Broadway Books, a division of Random House, Inc.

Visit our website at www.broadwaybooks.com

Library of Congress Cataloging-in-Publication Data
Lange, Gerry.
  Cain and Abel at work : how to overcome office politics and the people who stand between you and success / by Gerry Lange and Todd Domke.
    p. cm.
  ISBN 0-7679-0523-7
  1. Office politics. I. Domke, Todd. II. Title.

HF5386.5.L36 2001
650.1'3—dc21   00-062133
FIRST EDITION

Designed by Casey Hampton

01 02 03 04 05 10 9 8 7 6 5 4 3 2 1

Once again, with love, for C and C.

—G.W.L.

For Lance, Kirk, Parth, Laurel, and Lisa—Abels all.

—T.D.

ACKNOWLEDGMENTS

Special thanks to our literary agent, Margret McBride, her associate, Kris Sauer, and our incredible editor, Suzanne Oaks. We would also like to thank the dozens of people who shared their horror stories ("case studies") of Cains and Abels at work, but who wisely requested anonymity for fear of Cain retribution. Good luck to you all.

CONTENTS

◆ ◆ ◆

◆ ◆ ◆

Why Good Things Happen
to Bad People

The Bible tells us that Adam and Eve had two sons, Cain and Abel. Cain, jealous because God seemed to favor his brother, "rose up against Abel . . . and slew him." As punishment, God banished Cain, so Cain "went out from the presence of the LORD and dwelt in the land of Nod on the East of Eden" where he married and had a son, Enoch.

The moral of the Cain and Abel story seems to be that evil will be discovered and punished. But that's not entirely convincing. After all, Abel was dead, but Cain survived. He not only survived but seems to have done pretty well for himself. He courted and caught a wife and had a son—a nice, supportive, traditional nuclear family—and he also "built a city, and called the name of the city after the name of his son, Enoch."

So, it turns out that Cain was the first real estate developer, the Donald Trump of his time. And since Cain built a city and had the power to name it, we might also assume he ended up mayor of Enoch, making him also the first politician.

This unholy coalescing of business and politics by the Cains of this world is something that we have had ample opportunity to observe in our many years of experience in both fields. Over time, it has led us to ask a few simple questions about the way the world works—not how the world *ought* to work, not how religion and schools and motivational philosophies teach us the world *should* work, but how it all too often really works. Many business books have described what people do right to succeed; this book is about what people do wrong to succeed.

We use the names of the Old Testament characters Cain and Abel as a metaphor for the ongoing battle between cunning (Cain) and ability (Abel) in today's workplace. But make no mistake: What we are talking about is no mere metaphor. There are real Cains in "the real world." And, by the way, although we refer to Cains and Abels with only masculine pronouns—instead of saying "he or she" all the time—obviously we're talking about both sexes.

WHY YOU NEED THIS BOOK

Cains operate in every kind of organization—corporate, political, academic, military, even charitable. This book will help you spot these manipulative coworkers at an early stage—hopefully, before they can corner you, con you, and make your life miserable.

This is a book about the politics of business and the business of politics—a set of observations about how people often get ahead in the real world. From these observations we have abstracted the principles that explain why Cains often succeed, all too frequently at Abels' expense.

Why is it that many intelligent, hardworking people of ability don't get ahead faster? What is it that these Abels fail to understand about the world of business and politics? Why do some people of bad character and less ability succeed so well? What tactics do these Cains employ to slay Abels in the everyday world of business, politics, academia, and other pursuits?

In short, why do good things happen to bad people?

This book tries to answer that question.

For all the Abels of this world (and that is probably you), it is critical to understand who Cain is, how he operates, and why he is so often successful. And it is just as critical for Abel to understand himself—to recognize the qualities in himself that make him vulnerable to Cain's tactics.

You may not think of yourself as a naive innocent in competition with cunning rivals, but if you are concentrating on your work while a Cain is focused on promoting himself at your expense, you are vulnerable to his conniving gamesmanship.

Cain is a backstabber and a liar. He is a self-involved, manipulative, and ruthless individual. He aims to control people and situations for his own advantage and advancement, using a variety of tactics to accomplish his goals. Almost everyone has run across and been victimized by a Cain in the workplace. Sometimes, we recognize (usually too late) what Cain is up to, but much of the time Cain's maneuvering and manipulation are so skillful and subtle that they go unnoticed. Cain can be charming, and his tactics—stealing credit, placing blame, lying in many different ways—can be hard to detect. Because of this, Abel can be victimized without quite knowing how or by whom.

Abel feels at a disadvantage in office politics because he isn't a master of the game. *Cain and Abel at Work* gives Abel the information and insights to spot a Cain early on. Also, it will help any Abel become more aware of how his own trusting instincts can put him at risk of falling for the traps set by Cain. Recognizing and understanding Cain's behavior and Abel's own vulnerability are the keys to avoiding harmful, even career-ending mistakes. They are the keys to avoid becoming Cain's next victim.

So, this book serves as a warning, and warnings can be invaluable: Forewarned is forearmed. But it is more than just a warning. *Cain and Abel at Work* also gives you practical answers to questions like:

- How can I avoid confrontations with a Cain?
- What should I do if a Cain tries to steal credit that I deserve?
- When and how should I take action against a Cain?

WHAT YOU WILL LEARN

This book has five parts to it.

First, we answer the question: *Who is Cain?* We reveal the lies Cain tells, his lack of conscience, his consuming ambition, his drive for power, his bag of tricks, and his destructive greed.

Second, we consider *How to Spot Cain's Cons.* We focus on how he uses language (both spoken and written) and images to deceive people.

Third, we explore *Why Abel Is at Risk* of being exploited by Cain. We explain why Abel's upbringing and education do not truly prepare him to compete with a scheming Cain; how, in some ways, they actually mislead him about the true nature of a competitive world.

Fourth, in *Understanding Cain*, we look carefully at Cain and Abel in action, and we let three professional therapists offer different perspectives on why Cain is so self-serving.

Fifth, and finally, we examine *How to Cope with Cains*, and we describe twenty-seven keys for identifying and combatting Cain and his tactics. These keys can give Abel the knowledge and self-confidence to deal successfully with Cain's maneuverings. With the insights gained from this book, Abel can win a battle of survival with Cain without compromising himself. If you are an Abel yourself, then (to paraphrase the Ghost of Christmas Present in Dickens' *A Christmas Carol*) learn these lessons and learn them well. After all, if Abel had been watching his back, Cain might not have been able to sneak up and stab him in it.

ARE YOU MORE OF AN ABEL OR A CAIN?

Throughout the book, true-life examples are used to illustrate Cain's tactics. Many readers will find these stories all too familiar. Names, ages, gender, and other specifics have been altered in order to protect the sources from Cain's wrath, but the essential facts of the examples remain faithful in spirit.

At times in reading these case studies you will see a little more of yourself in the Cain character than in the Abel one. Does this mean you are a Cain? Not really. The fact is, there is some of Abel *and* Cain in all of us—the overweening ambition of Cain warring for dominance with the altruistic innocence of Abel. Few of us are 100 percent angel or 100 percent devil. When we call someone a "Cain" we are talking about someone within whom the Cain part dominates the Abel part, someone within whom corruption outweighs conscience. These individuals are few in number, but their influence and the harm they can do to others is too great to ignore.

So, as the song says, let's start at the very beginning, a very good place to start, by asking the question: Just who is this Cain? What is he like? What motivates him? How does he operate? And how can he live with himself?

1

· · ·

WHO

IS

CAIN?

❖ ❖ ❖

CHAPTER 1

The Lies Cains Tell

It would be a mistake to think of Cain as the reincarnation of Ivan the Terrible. He isn't obviously evil. If you're looking for someone overtly corrupt or conspicuously dishonest, you won't recognize Cain when you come across him. Nor would Cain recognize himself as such.

But Cain's ambitious nature *is* recognizable. Cain is so driven by ambition that he'll do almost anything to satisfy his lust for success. To get his way, he will use and manipulate others; he will stab an innocent colleague in the back, with no remorse; he will not only mislead those he works with, he will abuse them and make their lives miserable—and he will take pride in doing so. Why? Because he not only wants to advance himself and squelch any potential competition, he also wants and needs to prove to himself that he is superior in power and status.

But how does Cain live with himself? How can he act as he does and still face himself in the mirror? The answer is: Cain can live with himself because he lies to himself.

Cain is a master of the ultimate con artistry: self-deception.

The easiest and quickest lie is the one told to oneself. It only has to travel from one synapse to another, and is then buried forever in the subconscious.

To some degree, we all lie to ourselves. "Kidding ourselves" is a nice way to put it. But for Cain, self-deception is a basic operating mechanism.

This shamelessness is important to understanding Cain because few people can think of themselves as evil and behave in a self-confessed evil way. Remember, we are talking about "civilized" people—people who hold respectable jobs in business, government, and other institutions. We are not talking about violent psychopaths or discussing how the Borgias consolidated power by poisoning their rivals.

Besides, Cain isn't totally and self-consciously evil. He doesn't stride through life telling himself and the rest of the world how corrupt, venal, and unprincipled he is. That's a Hollywood script writer's stereotype about businessmen and politicians. It's the Gordon Gekko character in *Wall Street* ("Greed is good.") or any random business executive in a television program ("Look, I want to make a profit, and I don't care if we have to despoil the environment to do it"). Sometimes it seems as if television and screenwriters believe that the vast majority of murders in America are committed by the CEOs of the Fortune 500.

Much of the time, Cain will deal with people straightforwardly, fairly, and considerately. He might love his family and be genuinely close to a few friends. As Dean Martin crooned, everybody loves somebody sometime.

But when Cain sees an opportunity to get ahead, or when Cain's self-interest is threatened, then Abel, beware.

CASE STUDY 1

Arthur and Heather both worked in the public relations department of a large corporation, Heather as a writer, Arthur as the administrative assistant to the department head. Arthur was a Cain, always out for himself. He had schemed his way up the corporate ladder, and he lived by the motto, "Do unto others before they do unto you."

Heather was an Abel, always willing to help others when

they had trouble on the job. Her favorite saying was, "If you treat people fairly, they'll be fair with you."

One Friday afternoon, Ralph, a coworker, came to her with a problem. He had written some copy that was due by Monday for the corporation's new annual report, copy he thought was not only acceptable but good. However, he was convinced that their boss would reject his work out of hand. The boss had developed an intense dislike for Ralph, and on several occasions had thrown Ralph's work into the waste basket without even reading it, bouncing angrily in his large leather executive chair and shouting, "If this is from Ralph, it's garbage! Make him redo it."

Ralph had learned to accept all this as an unhappy fact of life, but this time he was agitated and distressed. As he sat before Heather, sweating and twisting his hands nervously, he told Heather that he and his wife were supposed to attend a family wedding out of state the following day, and if their boss rejected his work, he would be forced to skip the wedding and work all weekend rewriting copy to meet the Monday morning deadline. His wife had been looking forward to the event for months, and they had bought nonrefundable plane tickets. She would be brokenhearted if they had to cancel. Of course, she could always go by herself, but it wouldn't be the same.

"I just don't know what to do," Ralph said, "I just don't know what to do."

Heather sympathized.

"Look," she said, "I know he's irrational about your work. On the other hand, he thinks everything I do is a work of genius. Let me look over what you've done. If it needs any changes, I'll do a little editing, then I'll give it to him and not say anything about who wrote it."

Ralph was skeptical.

"But what if he asks?"

Heather thought for a moment. "If he asks, I'll tell him the truth: you wrote it, I looked it over, and made whatever changes I thought were necessary. As long as he thinks the final product has been rewritten by me, he'll accept it."

And it worked. Heather reviewed Ralph's copy, found that by and large it was at least passable, made a few minor changes, handed the copy to their boss (who declared it "A fine piece of work; not like that drivel Ralph writes"), and Ralph and his wife had a wonderful time at their family wedding.

Later, at an office gathering, Ralph mentioned the incident to Arthur, the Cain, who thought little of it but filed it away in his memory in case the information might prove useful in the future.

Arthur was ambitious in the extreme and was willing to do almost anything to advance his career. As the administrative assistant to the department head, he controlled the flow of information from middle managers to the boss. Whenever a particularly creative or well-reasoned idea fell into his hands, he would rephrase it slightly and pass it on to the head man as his own work.

For months, Arthur's scam worked, and worked well. Arthur was a fast-rising star and was amply rewarded with several raises for his unique "contributions" to the company. He bought a new Mercedes and treated himself to a week in Bermuda. Life was good—until the day Mary Beth, one of the middle managers, asked the department head what he thought about the proposal Mary Beth had submitted in her memo. The department head was taken aback and immediately asked someone to look into the matter.

When the investigator discovered the truth, well, the game was over. Arthur was called on the carpet to explain. This time it was Arthur who was sweating, searching frantically for some kind of defense. Then he remembered the story Ralph had told him.

"This kind of thing goes on all the time in this company," he told the boss. "For example, Heather has been claiming credit for work done by other people, work she never did."

The accusation against Heather didn't save Arthur's skin; he was fired. Heather and Ralph explained exactly what had happened to the investigator, who then reported everything to Heather's boss. Heather was severely reprimanded for her deception but managed to keep her job . . . for a while. When it became clear that her boss now distrusted her and had no intention of ever promoting her, she resigned her position.

Let's face it: Heather did nothing wrong in this case. She helped someone who was in trouble. That's all. Nothing she did threatened Arthur or even affected him in any way.

So, why did Arthur, the Cain, go after Heather in this case, especially since his accusation served no real purpose? He didn't have any particular grudge against her, and she wasn't a direct or even indirect rival of his.

The answer lies in Cain's fundamental nature.

- He routinely justifies his own conduct with the argument that "everyone does it."
- When cornered, he will strike out at others in the hope, no matter how remote, that the best defense is a good offense.
- He has no conscience in the normal sense of the word and is indifferent to the harm he causes innocent people. The only thing that matters to him is protecting himself.

This case illustrates a cardinal rule about working with a Cain:

◆ *THE VERY PRESENCE OF A CAIN AROUND YOU IS DANGEROUS.*

In extreme circumstances, Cain is willing to do almost anything, no matter how far-fetched or repugnant, to defend himself. If you are in the vicinity, you may get hit when he lashes out.

There is one other useful lesson to draw from this real-life case: If Ralph had kept quiet about what happened, neither he nor Heather would have become entangled in Arthur's scandal. Ralph's mistake was in volunteering information Arthur had no need to know. Heather's mistake was in failing to emphasize to Ralph how vital it was to keep this incident secret. Both failed to ask themselves two simple questions:

1. Is there any worthwhile purpose sharing potentially embarrassing stories with other people?
2. What are the possible consequences of someone else knowing about this story?

Abels tend to be open, candid, forthcoming people, qualities that serve them well when dealing with other Abels. But when dealing with Cains, these virtues can become faults. If you are an Abel, and you probably are, you should discipline yourself to ask the two questions mentioned above, even when you are convinced that you are surrounded by friends. Cain is clever enough and devious enough to fool most Abels into believing he can be trusted. And always remember this:

◆ *KNOWLEDGE IS POWER, AND IT IS CAIN'S NATURE TO MISUSE BOTH.*

Cain, in former president George Bush's awkward phrase, suffers from the "vision thing." His only real vision is the reflection he sees in the mirror. What is most real to him is his own self-interest, very narrowly defined as that which advances him in gaining power, money, status, and admiration.

Cain isn't restrained by any kind of intrusive morality, i.e., a conscience. He suppresses it in ways that wouldn't work for Abel, who would be too self-aware and embarrassed to fool himself so easily. But self-deception is fundamental to Cain; it is the necessary condition that allows Cain to connive, cheat, cut corners, conspire . . . all to raise Cain.

In this respect, Abel is the true opposite of Cain. Abel often feels guilty. He may feel guilty about not getting to work earlier or not staying later, about not working harder, about taking a sick day when he isn't sick, about taking an extra-long lunch hour, about nearly anything. Interestingly, although we use the pronoun "he," women are far more likely than men to suffer from this gnawing sense of guilt, perhaps because society's expectations impose an array of obligations on women—from child care to looking after an elderly parent—without expecting, let alone demanding, nearly as much from men.

EVERYONE ELSE IS DOING IT, SO WHY CAN'T I?

Earlier we said that there is some of both Cain and Abel in all of us. Cain stretches that small truth into a universal rationalization: "Everybody is like me. Everybody does what I do. I'm just better at it." No one, even Cain, likes to think that he is the worst person around, the only one acting deviously. So Cain lies to himself about others.

Cain's assertion, of course, is fundamentally cynical. It is an allegation of group guilt and, consequently, group responsibility, a notion that inevitably erodes the idea of individual responsibility. Everybody's doing it, so no one, especially Cain, is responsible for any of it.

Expedient justification is related to universal rationalization. If people are basically like Cain, then it isn't really immoral to exploit them.

CASE STUDY 2

A buyer toured a small factory that manufactured one of the components used by the buyer's company to make its products. He was escorted by the factory manager. The working conditions were deplorable; the air was barely breathable, no windows for light. It was unbearably hot inside the plant. The workers looked dirty, haggard, and, needless to say, depressed. Their wages were shockingly low.

"This place makes Dante's Inferno look like Club Med," the buyer thought to himself.

When one worker asked the manager if he could take a water break, the manager barked at him, "Go ahead . . . but if you do, don't bother coming back!"

It reminded the buyer of Oliver Twist begging for some more gruel, and it gnawed at the buyer's conscience, until he finally had to say something.

"How in hell do you get anyone to work in this place? You couldn't pay me enough to take a job here."

The manager shrugged.

"Half these guys probably sneaked across the border last week. If they weren't doing this, they'd either be sitting in the shade somewhere taking a siesta, making zilch, or they'd be lying drunk in the gutter. Besides, they don't last more than sixty days anyway."

As with universal rationalization ("Everybody's doing it"), expedient justification is rooted in cynicism, an attitude essential for Cain to maintain some feeling of self-respect.

In his own mind, Cain has to debase and devalue others in order to justify taking advantage of them. He convinces himself that other people *deserve* to be exploited because they are, by his own definition, either stupid or, like Cain himself, dishonest and manipulative. Cain may not be content with convincing himself; he may resort to ridiculing Abel (behind Abel's back) in an attempt to further justify his own feelings and behavior by needling others into agreeing with his opinion of Abel.

This intrinsic cynicism also makes Cain a firm believer that the end justifies the means, at least as far as he's concerned.

CASE STUDY 3

A political candidate had a carefully cultivated public image: honest, ethical, conscientious. Over the years, he had always taken the "good" side of every issue, the "moral" side, the "right" side. Like Superman, he stood for "Truth, Justice, and the American Way." He was widely admired for his rectitude and trustworthiness.

In truth, his instinct for political survival had far more to do with his political stances than any sense of personal honor. His moral compass always pointed to whatever was popular and expedient.

During one of his runs for reelection, when he was being challenged by a well-known and well-financed opponent, he was offered a sizable campaign contribution by an "investment advisor." The candidate's political consultants warned him to turn it down because the donor had a shady past.

"What did he do?" the candidate asked.

"Embezzlement," he was told. "The guy cheated some old people out of their savings with a phony investment scheme."

The candidate was still reluctant to turn down the money; in his mind, he needed it to offset his opponent's personal wealth.

"Was the guy convicted of anything?"

"No," the consultants admitted, "but he's been sued all over the place."

The candidate still wouldn't give up, "What did the courts say?"

"Well, he's managed to tie up the cases in court for more than three years. The way things are going, there may never be a final decision."

The candidate was finally satisfied. "Well, then, I'm taking the money; it's not as if he killed anybody."

Ultimately, Cain's cynicism breeds paranoia. His contempt for the morality of others makes him continually suspicious of their motivations, which, in turn, helps him justify in his own mind whatever nasty tactics he must employ to "protect" himself. Cain is in a continuous feedback loop: Cynicism engenders universal rationalization and expedient justification leading to paranoia that breeds even greater cynicism, all of which reinforces the cycle.

Cain is more paranoid than Abel could ever imagine because, as Cain sees it, he is competing with other Cains, who are just as devious and ruthless as himself. And he suspects everybody. If, occasionally, he comes to believe that someone is actually an Abel—an innocent—this doesn't ease his paranoia because Abels are still "players" to him, albeit just pawns.

One way to identify a Cain is by his concern about who knows who. Cain always thinks in terms of alliances and sponsors because of his assumption that advancement is based on connections rather than ability and performance. For example, if someone is being considered for promotion or a new job, Abel will ask, "Can she do the job?" But Cain will wonder, "Who does she know? Who recommended her?"

Because of how he thinks and behaves, Cain often creates real enemies—people who are "out to get him." Others may have no reasonable alternative if they wish to protect themselves. In other words, Cain's paranoia becomes self-fulfilling. Cain's behavior forces others around him to act like himself, which, to Cain, proves that his cynicism is both an accurate and justified view of human nature.

MEMORY LOSS

Cain also has a convenient memory. For example, he may come to believe that an idea proposed by someone else actually originated with him. He isn't pretending to believe this; he actually does believe it.

This is a second kind of self-lie, a way of changing reality to serve Cain's purposes by rewriting history. In some ways, it is the most destructive kind of lie; it makes it possible for Cain to completely ignore his worst behavior because it never happened. Cain never has to face up to what he actually did and to the consequences of his actions because in his mind he never did anything wrong.

A corollary of this is that Cain never self-corrects his immoral behavior from experience because in his own mind the experience is nothing to be embarrassed about or ashamed of.

A more subtle form of this memory-loss self-lie is Cain's ability to change his views as often as it suits his self-interest. He may be aware of his shifting stands, but he can easily suppress any embarrassment about his inconsistency because he doesn't really care about ideas or principles except insofar as they affect his own advancement. Past beliefs and positions are discarded as if they never existed.

CASE STUDY 4

A political candidate was involved in a tough run for reelection. She was a liberal with a history of "principled" opposition to the death penalty.

During the past year, several sensational murders had occurred in her district: a policeman had been shot down in cold blood; a young child had been kidnapped, raped, and strangled; and a young woman had disappeared from a dance club, her nude, dismembered body found three days later stuffed in a dumpster.

The candidate's opponent, a conservative, was hammering away at the death penalty issue, and polling indicated that the opponent was gaining ground.

In a staff meeting, the worried candidate was thinking aloud. "Maybe I could come out in support of the death penalty for cop killers. That might help blunt the issue."

Her issues director stared at her in disbelief. "You would support the death penalty for cop killers, right?" he asked.

"That's right," she answered. "What do you think?"

"I think you should answer this question: Why do you support it for someone who kills a cop, but not for someone who rapes and murders a three-year-old child?"

The candidate had a ready answer. "Because the cop has an especially dangerous job. He's vulnerable."

"Interesting," the issues advisor replied. "So, you don't think the three-year-old child who was kidnapped, raped, and strangled was vulnerable?"

The candidate waved her arms frantically. "That's not what I said! Of course the three-year-old was vulnerable."

"So, you support the death penalty for the man who killed the three-year-old?"

"I suppose I could."

"What about a four-year-old?"

"There's no real difference."

"A five-year-old?"

The candidate didn't answer.

"A twenty-year-old girl who was dismembered?"

The candidate sat silent. She obviously had no answer.

The candidate had no answer because she hadn't really thought about the issue in any terms other than political expediency. She wasn't concerned with the principles involved, just the principal involved.

Cain not only changes his views to suit his self-interest, he has within himself what we might call an incompatibility capacity—an ability to hold contradictory views without the slightest twinge of self-consciousness or intellectual mortification. It is a kind of short-term memory loss where previous beliefs can be rapidly abandoned and then, if necessary, embraced again.

Cain can pretend to agree with every side in a dispute because he doesn't really care which is right. He can reconcile opposites in his own mind because he gauges right/wrong, good/bad points of view by whether agreeing with one or the other is most useful to himself, and the answer to this question can change depending on who Cain is talking to at a given moment.

Cain is always happiest when he can convince *every* side in a disagreement that he is their ally. He wants everyone to perceive him as a friend and supporter. This guarantees that he will be on the winning side no matter what the outcome. As an added bonus, the losing side(s) will still regard him favorably because, after all, he did champion their viewpoint.

MOTIVATION FABRICATION

Cain not only lies to himself about others, he also lies to himself about his own motivations. He often rationalizes that the success he craves and the tactics he uses to achieve it are really for the benefit of others, not for himself. If patriotism is the last refuge of a scoundrel, then for Cain, family, friends, company, and coworkers are the first. Here again, Cain comes to believe his own lie. Nevertheless, it is a lie. Cain is willing to sacrifice family, the affection of his friends, the welfare of his employer, and the respect of his fellow workers to advance his own self-interest.

Cain will often tell anyone who's listening, "It's not the money," or "I don't care about the power." Like light bouncing off a mirror, Cain's words are a reversed image of what he really cares about, and what he assumes everyone else cares about. Cain can't help but believe that others are motivated by the most venal desires since these are the cravings of his own ambition. In denying his true motivations, he makes himself superior to everyone else in his own mind, and this reinforces his sense that his own behavior is justified.

Always keep this in mind: If a Cain tells you that it's not the money or it's not the power, then it's the money or the power.

Cain is not only a con man, he's a conflicted man. He needs to keep himself conned while still appraising every detail of every situation realistically and opportunistically. This is what makes Cain more complex than Abel, and, like most villains, more interesting.

A word of warning here: Even if you feel that you understand a Cain, don't back him into a corner and let him know that you see through him. If you interfere with his lie, you disrupt his self-esteem and threaten his sense of security, which comes in part from his confidence that no one knows what he's really up to. Cain can't let you get away with knowing his dirty little secret. Regardless of how you handle it, Cain will twist what you say in his own mind and project it onto you. He will mark you as an enemy, and, as you may recall, that didn't work out too well for Cain's brother.

◈ ◈ ◈

CHAPTER 2

Cain's Moral Indifference;
Or, in a Rat Race, the Rat Wins

In the last chapter we described how Cain is able to live with himself because he lies to himself about his own motivations and behavior. But not even Cain can lie to himself all the time. Sometimes, even if only semiconsciously, he has to face the reality and consequences of his actions—the harm that he's unfairly caused someone else or the fact that he has received a reward he doesn't deserve.

What happens then?

Pretty much nothing.

Because unlike Abel, Cain feels little or no guilt about what he does. Abel cares about the effects of his actions on others, and this caring (guilt, if you wish) acts as a check on his behavior. Cain doesn't. His attitude is summed up in a comment that boxing champion Sugar Ray Robinson once made: "Hurting people is my business." Cain may talk about "competition," but he means the same thing.

This is the "indifference difference" between Cain and Abel. Abel cares about how he affects others; Cain doesn't.

As we will explain, Cain is addicted to power. He takes it seriously and craves it. His measure of himself is his "success" in business as measured by externalities. Of course, Abel also wants to be successful. Who doesn't? But on this score, there is a quantitative difference between Cain and Abel so great that it amounts to a qualitative one. As someone once pointed out, in a breakfast of ham and eggs, both the chicken and the pig play a role, but the chicken is involved while the pig is committed.

Abel is *involved* with himself and with success; Cain is *committed* to both.

If you haven't run across even one Cain in your life, chances are that you haven't had much experience with power politics in a corporation, association, or political campaign. Maybe you've just been lucky. Or perhaps you are an Abel innocent to a fault and simply haven't recognized the Cains around you. Abels often have trouble believing that anyone can be as scheming and as amoral as Cain can in fact be. Abel often makes the mistake of thinking that Cain, when caught misbehaving, will learn from his mistake and reform himself. What Cain learns, instead, is not to get caught making that particular mistake again. What else do you expect? He's a success zealot and isn't about to abandon his obsession.

SELF-INTEREST VERSUS SELFISH INTEREST

The ultimate reality to Cain is his self-interest, narrowly defined.

All of us act out of self-interest. In fact, a usually reliable rule is that you can trust someone only as far as his self-interest goes. But this begs the question: How does a person define self-interest? It is a safe guess that Saddam Hussein's definition differs considerably from the Pope's definition.

Now, some people will immediately succumb to the facile argument so seductive to college freshmen in an introductory philosophy course. It is the simplistic logic that reasons this way: Both Saddam and the Pope are doing what makes them happiest, and, therefore, both are acting out of "selfish" motives.

But most of us recognize that some distinctions are true differences. Like the Pope, Abel's definition of self-interest incorporates a certain amount of selflessness; that is, he values doing good for other people, or at least not doing bad to them. There may be an element of this in

Cain's definition of self-interest, but only when doing good for others or not doing them harm can be accomplished without in any way affecting Cain's own selfish self-interest. Again, this may only be a difference of degree between Cain and Abel, but the gap is so sizable that for all practical purposes it is really a difference of kind—an "indifference difference."

Cain is so indifferent to the welfare of others that when he hears of a colleague's untimely death, he instinctively analyzes how he might profit from the loss. Without guilt or shame, he ponders the possibilities. Can he gain more power? A promotion? A pay raise? A better parking spot?

THE LYIN' KING

Cain may lie, cheat, and maneuver only when it's necessary. The problem is that Cain routinely sees it as "necessary." For self-protection, he has to use the same techniques as everyone around him, and, of course, he assumes that those around him are frequently lying, cheating, and maneuvering. After all, if he were in their place, this is what he would be doing.

Cain always has a goal of more power and prestige for himself and is constantly plotting a way to reach this goal. Almost nothing slows him down; certainly not morality. He not only enjoys working toward his goal, he also enjoys the intensity of the finagling along the way. Intrigue is emotionally satisfying for him, especially if he ultimately wins. If others get hurt in the process, well, that's their fault. They shouldn't get in his way.

There are times when it seems as if Cain actually prefers cheating, even if there is a safe, honest way to achieve his goal.

CASE STUDY 5

Spencer was an aide to a presidential appointee. He had previously served as a top business consultant. Spencer was on a fast track to the top in Washington and planned to spend only a year or two in his present position, then leave to set himself up as a private lobbyist. In his first year as a lobbyist, Spencer expected to have an income of more than $300,000.

In the meantime, however, he was feeling financially pinched by his government salary because he had a wife and children to support. Neither Spencer nor his wife trusted day care. Both strongly believed that their children would be better off if she could stay at home and watch over their children, at least until they were old enough to go to school.

To solve their problem, Spencer thought up a cute scheme. He used his White House position to put his wife on the payroll. His wife had a no-show job, which allowed her to stay home with their children while being paid by the government.

The irony is that Spencer had a perfectly reasonable alternative for dealing with his financial pressures. Because of the positions he had held, he had very good personal contacts with several extremely wealthy people who owed him favors, any one of whom would have been willing to lend him whatever he needed on ludicrously generous terms, e.g., low interest on the loan, payable over twenty years, no payments to begin until he left government service and secured a job in the private sector or established his own business (when he would be making enough so that repayment would be negligible).

So why run the risk he did?

This is the kind of question Abel asks himself . . . and can't answer because he has trouble understanding Cain's preference for deception.

One possible answer is that Cain takes a kind of sadistic joy in "putting one over" on the world. He experiences a rush of excitement in getting away with his cheating. The more Cain cuts corners, the more he feels the thrill of winning, as if in cutting corners he's passing his competitors in the rat race. Victory is all the more satisfying because it is the climax of shrewd scheming.

Cain is not only indifferent to people, he is indifferent to accepted morality—a sort of thinking that isn't within Abel's life experiences or consciousness.

GRUESOME'S LAW

Gresham's Law says that bad currency drives good currency out of circulation. A Cain in the workplace gives rise to Gruesome's Law:

◆ *BAD BEHAVIOR IS CONTAGIOUS AND DRIVES OUT GOOD BEHAVIOR.*

Over time, Cain's behavior infects others. It creates a general behavioral pollution that suffuses the business environment; everyone is forced to act like Cain out of sheer survival instincts. Collegiality is replaced by cabals, intrigue, conspiracy, and paranoia.

For any business, this is the very real threat presented by Cain: eventually, his actions undermine morale and productivity.

Cain himself cares little for the overall health of the enterprise. He would rather risk harming the company than resign himself to less than personal "victory."

One of Cain's greatest strengths is this ability to force others to play his game. It is a game he's good at, and, consequently, a game he is likely to win. Cain's actions are guided not only by the Law of the Jungle, but by the Law of the Rodent:

◆ *IN A RAT RACE, A RAT WINS.*

* * *

CHAPTER 3

Cain's Drive for Power

To Abel, Cain is an enigma. Abel often recognizes that Cain is ambitious and driven, and he may sense that Cain isn't to be wholly trusted, but he really can't figure him out. Even when Abel thinks he understands Cain, he usually doesn't, because Cain's ego, his insecurity, and his fundamental amorality are alien to Abel's own personality and values. Abel's high school civics view of how the world works never prepared him for anyone like Cain.

In trying to understand Cain, we don't propose to psychoanalyze him; still, for Abel's sake, we can draw Cain's basic profile, emphasizing the most important attributes of his character.

And the most important of all is this:

◆ **CAIN CRAVES POWER.**

"Power is his ideology, his friend, his concubine, his mistress, his passion. Everything beyond that, beyond the struggle for power, concerns him much less."

This was said about onetime Russian President Boris Yeltsin by a former staffer, and it is a fitting description of Cain as well.

Unlike Abel, who concentrates on doing his job, Cain thinks constantly about power—how to get it, how to preserve it, how to expand it, how to use it for his own purposes. For Cain, power is an art form. But it is also more than that; the love and pursuit of power is at the core of his survival instinct. He needs power, because for him it is an emotional and mental addiction.

This obsession with power shouldn't be confused with authority. Authority implies a legitimate stewardship over others based on the assumption that you work with people to accomplish a common goal. In Cain's drive for power, people are mere objects to be manipulated for personal ambition. For example, power can justify keeping the wrong person in the wrong job if it serves Cain's agenda, such as undermining a rival's performance and reputation. If Cain were an honest steward of the authority invested in him, he couldn't justify to himself a decision which clearly undermines the interests of the employee and the organization.

But Cain isn't an honest steward of authority. To repeat, Cain is interested in two things: power and himself. To understand what this means in the everyday behavior of Cain and Abel, consider the following comparison:

WHILE ABEL THINKS IN TERMS OF . . .	CAIN THINKS IN TERMS OF . . .
problems facing the organization	problems facing him, e.g., threats to his position
getting the job done	getting credit, title, status, perks for doing the job
teamwork	power over others, i.e., turf
loyalty to colleagues	subordinates' loyalty to him
accountability	avoiding blame
competitors	enemies
corporate campaign goals	personal promotion

Abel believes that power comes from his ability to work with others and from within himself—from his internal values, talents, and knowledge. Cain, though, sees power as external: "What budget do I control? How big is my office? What is my job title? How many people work under me? Where's my name on the office distribution list? How does my salary compare to others? Do I have my own parking space, and how far is it from the front door?"

The most discouraging thing of all is how often these shallow, external symbols of success impress others, even Abel. It is difficult for anyone to be entirely indifferent to things that telegraph wealth, status, and privilege. Ask yourself this question: How do you perceive a coworker who has an impressive title, a bigger office than yours, and a reserved parking space near the front entrance?

Abel finds fulfillment in accomplishment, family, faith—something other than self-aggrandizement. Cain's is the extremely ego-driven life of an insecure person for whom self-worth comes from money, power, and recognition. He looks to salary, office, and title because they tell him where he stands in the office hierarchy; they are his reality and security.

Cain is the quintessential territorial animal. To him, success is a zero-sum game. He feels that if you're up, he's down . . . diminished relative to you. The idea of win/win is alien to him. He truly, deeply, madly prefers a win/lose system because it's crucial to him that his enemies lose. Cain doesn't feel secure if others around him don't feel insecure.

This is why power-seeking is an integral part of his survival instinct. He needs power to feel important. The accomplishments and success of others mean that someone else may be rising at his expense, that attention and credit are going to someone other than himself, that promotions and the power that accompanies them may be given to others. Cain is always acutely conscious of his rivals, and he routinely schemes to put roadblocks in their way.

It is often said that a successful executive is one who prepares those below him on the corporate ladder to do his job. But Cain makes certain that nobody under him is in a position to take his job. If Cain feels threatened by a subordinate's ability, he may well try to maneuver the subordinate into failure, perhaps by transferring him to a dead-end job, perhaps by handing him a "land mine" assignment. Cain's power mentality has an inner voice always warning him: "Watch out for that guy. Better get him out of the way."

CASE STUDY 6

A computer company had an in-house department that designed its documents. The department was weak and did uninspired work, and upper management began talking quietly with an outside firm about taking over its functions.

George, a young and upcoming executive with the computer company, learned about the unit's shaky future. He approached the company's CEO about Dwight, one of his staffers whom he considered a potential rival. "Dwight is incredibly talented," he told the CEO. "He's the perfect guy to head up the design department."

The CEO was impressed with George's recommendation and took his advice. Dwight was named design manager and thanked George profusely for his thoughtful support. "There aren't many people who would go out of their way to help someone else like that," he told George.

"Believe me, you deserved it," George said.

When the department was abolished six months later, so was the potential rival. He was out of a job.

A few weeks later, George treated the despondent Dwight to dinner and commiserated with him: "That's the problem with companies today; no damn loyalty."

Cain's idea of loyalty is peculiar, and very different from Abel's. If some new idea or proposed change arises within a corporation, Abel wants to know, "How does it affect the company?" Cain wants to know, "How does it affect me?"

Ironically, this difference in perspective may give Cain a significant advantage over Abel in office politics. He is immediately focused on how best to position himself in the new environment so that his superiors will perceive him as a successful executive. Cain understands that it is much easier to achieve narrow, short term goals for yourself than longer-term goals for the corporation.

Let's review some of the obvious contrasts between Cain and Abel:

Abel is an organization man.	Cain is a self-server who is adept at looking like an organization man.
Abel respects subordinates.	Cain loves subservience.
Abel enjoys achievement.	Cain craves the prestige that comes from getting credit for achievement.

Abel may sleep better at night, but Cain would never change places with him. He considers Abel's outlook on life both dull and unrealistic. For Cain, life is a struggle for power that ends in defeat or victory. His philosophy was summed up by Lucifer in Milton's *Paradise Lost*:

> *To reign is worth ambition, though in hell:*
> *Better to reign in hell than serve in heav'n.*

While Cain may hide his lust for power from most Abels, he will often do the opposite with other Cains. Without saying so explicitly, he will warn them, "Keep off my turf. I'm serious about my ambitions, so don't try anything that threatens my status." In effect, it's one con man signaling another.

When it serves their mutual benefit, Cains will sometimes form short-term alliances with each other. So long as their interests coincide, they can make a formidable team, protecting one another when necessary, combining to torpedo rivals when possible. In most cases, however, there will be an eventual falling out because at some point it is advantageous for one of them to double-cross the other, so he will.

Cain's ethos was nicely summed up by W. C. Fields: "If a thing is worth having, it's worth cheating for."

* * *

CHAPTER 4

Cain's Measure of Success; Or, Ability Is in the Eye of the Beholder

We use Cain and Abel as a metaphor to illustrate that *cunning* often slays *ability* in the workplace. But how does Cain himself see this competition? Well, since Cain lies to himself about a great many things, it should come as no surprise that he views his own cunning *as* ability.

To Cain, winning is the most important value; it's everything. Therefore, he considers anything that helps him win as inherent ability. Others may call his tactics deceptive; he calls them shrewd. Others may say he's manipulative; he says he's just result-oriented. Others may argue that he relies on office politics; he counters that they are just jealous of his people skills.

Is ability in the eye of the beholder a matter of perception rather than reality? Cain, cynically, believes so. This is why he tries to position himself as the one who beholds.

For nearly everyone in the business world, the most consequential definition of ability is the definition held by those immediately above you in the chain of command and, therefore, in the chain of promotion or other reward.

In other words, the person who defines ability is critical.

And ability can be difficult to define, even under the best of circumstances where there is general agreement about how to measure it.

CASE STUDY 7

Jack and Jill are both salespeople. They work for the same company and sell the same items to the same sorts of clients. The geographic territories they cover are alike, both physically and demographically. Jack, however, successfully completes 50 percent of the sales calls he makes, while Jill completes only 20 percent—and Jack averages $100 in sales per call, Jill only $50.

Who would you hire as your sales person if you were a businessman and needed one?

Would your answer change in light of the following information? Jack is the brother-in-law of the manager who determines sales assignments. The manager assigns Jack only established clients—those who have a previous history of purchasing products from Jack's company; Jill only handles prospective clients, new buyers.

Then add this fact: According to data compiled by the company, 70 percent of established clients repurchase items from the company, and these repurchases average $200 in orders per call; only 10 percent of potential new clients purchase, averaging $25 per call.

By these measures, Jack is averaging 20 percent fewer repurchases than the average salesperson and $100 less than average per purchase. Jill is more than twice as successful as the average salesperson in recruiting new clients, and she's bringing in orders that are double the average for these clients. Whose record really suggests more ability?

The answer seems obvious, yet much of the time people will still answer "Jack" because the existence of an apparently objective standard—in this case, an easily understood number—seduces their judgment. Oh, they may pay lip service to the fact that Jill has done better than expected . . . but there's still that glaring statistic that says Jack is selling more than Jill.

So, people often make judgments about ability based on what they most easily understand.

They also judge ability on instinctive reactions to "qualities" that may have little or nothing to do with accomplishment or getting a job done.

Personality, appearance, relationships, and other such subjective characteristics may overwhelm every other consideration. In even the best-run corporations, competent executives are passed up for promotion because a rival has personal connections that trump superior credentials, ability, and accomplishments.

JUDICIAL INCOMPETENCE

One of the most annoying frustrations faced by Abel is that he will often be judged by superiors who are incompetent judges of ability or accomplishment. This is because businessmen frequently see "management ability" as a unique talent separate from and superior to other abilities, so someone perceived as having good management ability can end up directing and evaluating people who are performing jobs that the manager himself is incompetent to do.

CASE STUDY 8

Martha had a job writing manuals for a major corporation. She had earned a master's degree in English and had received straight As in her English composition courses. In her senior year, she had been elected to the literature and language honor society.

Her boss had majored in business courses as an undergraduate and had attended a business school, where he learned to walk the executive walk and talk the executive talk. He looked, sounded, dressed, and acted like a "manager." As a student, he had taken the minimum number of English and literature credits and had avoided courses requiring much composition because he knew that his writing abilities were extremely weak. As a freshman, he had actually failed and had to retake the required introductory English course at his college. At work itself, he never wrote anything, even a short memo. He always had his administrative assistant submit a draft, which he then "critiqued," usually with fatuous comments.

"Use a different font. I don't like the look of this one."

"Put this in italics and that in bold."

"Make this punchier. You know, use smaller words."

All the while, he knew that his superiors were watching to see whether he was really a "take charge" kind of guy (i.e., a true "manager").

Whenever Martha submitted a manual for approval, this manager ripped it apart and demanded extensive changes, most of which were not only wrongheaded but downright ungrammatical. But he knew that by demanding changes, he was demonstrating managerial "guidance" and "decisiveness."

The manager was always highly critical of Martha's work and gave her mediocre performance reviews and minimal pay raises.

Martha became so fed up that when the manager made the mistake of finally putting something in writing and sent her a two-page memo in his own words, she blue-penciled it, marking more than sixty syntactical, grammatical, punctuation, spelling, and sentence fragment errors in the fewer than one hundred lines of the communication. She then photocopied her edited version and circulated copies of it throughout the company.

Needless to say, Martha was soon looking for another job.

THE QUALITY OF QUANTITY

In most cases, Abel wants judgments to be based on output; Cain wants judgments to be based on input. Cain doesn't want a system where advancement is based on the quality of ideas or the quality of work. Cain wants to create a work environment where quantity has a quality all its own.

For example, Cain is often willing to work long hours. He may be the first to arrive at work and the last to leave. He may be willing to work holidays, and he may rarely, if ever, take vacations. These are exactly the kinds of sacrifices that Cain is willing to make: hours, family, community affairs. This standard gives Cain an edge in his battle with Abel.

There is an enormous gap between the rhetoric and actions of many managers when it comes to the input/output equation, illustrated by the following.

CASE STUDY 9

In the Nixon White House, one of the President's ranking aides incessantly stressed that he cared most about the quality of work produced by his staff. One of his favorite stories—maybe apocryphal—concerned the physicist, Niels Bohr.

Bohr, it seems, was once asked by a nuclear power company to examine a malfunctioning reactor. Bohr studied the problem for five minutes, walked over to the reactor, turned a few knobs, and the machine hummed into action. Later, he submitted a bill for $10,000.

The company wrote back asking for an itemized account. Bohr sent a new bill: "Turning knobs: $1.00. Knowing which knobs to turn: $9,999.00."

It was a cute story, but the staff paid little attention to its supposed lesson because they knew that their boss didn't believe a word of it. In fact, he was someone who lived for his work. He came to the office seven days a week, arriving before anyone else and leaving late at night. His wife and three young children rarely saw him. In fact, he was such a stranger to his two-year-old that whenever (during one of his rare appearances at home) he went to pick up little Timmy to play, the child would cry violently and demand to be returned to the arms of his mother.

At work, despite his professed belief in the *quality* of his staff's work, he was a tyrant about hours. He never complimented anyone on the excellence of their work, and he viciously berated any staffer who came in after 7 A.M. or left before 9 P.M. Clearly, he most valued how much time someone put in on the job, regardless of how good or bad a job they did while there.

Some staff members were so terrified by his demands that if they had to get away early for any reason, they would leave their office lights on and place open briefcases on their desks to give the impression they were still at work. A few of the men kept extra suit jackets hidden away so they could hang them over the backs of their desk chairs to further the illusion.

Of course, in many cases, the quantity of output may be a legitimate measure of an employee's contribution to the company, and the quantity of output may be a function of the quantity of input. By their very nature, some jobs demand long hours; managing a start-up company, for example, isn't a 9-to-5 job five days a week. In some cases, a company's revenues may be closely related to hours worked by employees: The more billable hours an attorney works, the more money he earns for his firm.

In both of these cases, however, there is a danger that the quality of work will decline in proportion to hours worked because of fatigue or "burnout."

And there is the even greater danger that the need for, or emphasis placed on, input will become the only standard for judging performance—something that, as we said, is all too often the case.

Interestingly, where objective measures of success exist, ability—as measured by output and quality of work—is more likely to become the dominant standard. Actors are paid not on the basis of how many hours they work but on a predicted likelihood of how much money their film will gross based on past performance. Of course, "ability" here refers to proven success at attracting a large audience to your films, not to some critic's abstract notion of "talent."

THE SUCCESS OF FAILURE

Cain knows that failure can sometimes be judged a demonstration of ability, which is surely one of the oddest truths about "competence" as reckoned in the "real" world. This phenomenon usually occurs in jobs high up in the corporate organization, where specialized knowledge or experience is limited to a very few people; CEOs are one example. After all, how many people in the entire country have experience in managing large corporations?

In most cases, when a large corporation dismisses one of its highest-ranking executives for failing at his or her job, the executive is quickly picked up by some other large corporation. Why? Because this executive has "done it before." He or she has the "experience" necessary to do the job (even if it was done badly for someone else).

Some might argue that this isn't about ability; it's about experience. But this is a distinction without a difference. The end result is that the dismissed CEO is rehired because of a perception that he or she can do the job better than other available candidates.

The success of failure is a limited principle that works only where the universe of potential competitors is extremely small. In other words, where demand exceeds supply. But it is also a principle that is expanding its influence because of corporate fear. Most corporations today shy away from offering any kind of recommendation, pro or con, about former employees applying for new jobs. Businesses dread being sued for unfavorable comments (a sensible fear given modern juries) and avoid the risk by refusing to disclose performance reviews and by ordering current employees to deny requests for information. This means that actual performance drops out of the picture, and a prospective employer is left to judge candidates solely by the fact that they have experience doing a similar job. If this trend continues, many corporations will hire successful failures, and the success of failure may become the rule not the exception.

So, are we now living in a bizarre world where failure is success, wrong is right, and ability is solely in the eye of a biased beholder? Hopefully not. But let's be realistic in recognizing that a Cain will *try* to pervert the way that success is measured in an organization. He doesn't want personal advancement to be based on the quality of one's ideas or work, but rather based primarily on the "ability" to be opportunistic, deceptive, crafty, and ruthless. In other words, he wants advancement to be based on what he's best at.

. . .

CHAPTER 5

Cain's Calculating Caution

People generally prefer to keep doing what they are comfortable doing, and what they are most comfortable doing is what they have been doing. Most people dislike change and tend to resist new ideas or any significant alteration in the way they do their jobs. This can be stated as a simple principle:

⬥ *FAMILIARITY HAS MOMENTUM.*

Cain has a clear understanding of the Momentum of the Familiar, which is why he looks for assignments that are conventional, easily accomplished, and where success can be demonstrated by a simple, "objective" standard. Innovators, on the other hand, are usually Abels. When they see an opportunity to do something better for the company, they tend to pursue it, even at the risk of becoming a "pest" in the eyes of management.

CASE STUDY 10

Ken was an engineer and a product representative for a company that manufactured flexible hoses for industrial use.

Whenever he visited potential clients, he would spend time discussing their needs and the ways in which his company could help meet them. It soon became clear that many of the clients needed a specific kind of bellows for certain applications, and they were willing to pay a fair price for such a device.

Ken returned to company headquarters and reported what he had learned. After hearing his pitch, higher-ups explained that the company was in the business of flexible hoses, not bellows, and besides, no one really knew how to make a workable and affordable bellows like the one Ken was talking about.

Ken was sent back into the field with his hoses, where once again he was told, "We need special bellows."

Back to home base, where he was rejected again . . . and again . . . and again.

After several years and many rejections, Ken was fed up. He finally told his bosses, "Look, if you aren't interested in the bellows, I am. I'm going to quit and find a way of making these things." With a roll of their eyes and a limp pat on the back, Ken's bosses let him go. They didn't worry much about competition since they were sure "it couldn't be done." Around the company, they joked about "Ken's Folly."

Ken went to his wife and told her that he had quit his job because he had confidence in his idea and in himself. He wanted to use their savings and money borrowed from friends and family to set up a machine shop in his garage where he could work on his invention. His wife and everyone else were worried about the chance he was taking, but his enthusiasm and belief in himself convinced enough of them—he raised the money he needed. For two years, he toiled away in his garage, night and day, but he succeeded.

Ken secured a patent on his invention and built a successful company to produce and market it. "Ken's Folly" made him more than a hundred million dollars. In the meantime, his previous employers went out of business.

Just having a good idea doesn't guarantee success, of course. Entrepreneurs fail all the time. In this instance, Ken not only had access to special information, he also had very good judgment. Moreover, he had extraordinary skill. Most people don't. Indeed, most Abels would have failed in his venture, while Cain, by playing it safe, would have remained in his job with an opportunity to advance himself because his bosses were drifting, carried along by the momentum of the familiar.

Inefficiency and missed opportunities are an affront to Abel's self-esteem because he takes pride in his ability. By contrast, inefficiency is irrelevant to Cain unless it affects his own position or chance for advancement.

One reason for including this case study here is to illustrate the strong romantic appeal of working for yourself, playing the lone genius, building your own company, and making a fortune. It is a wonderful dream—one that often succeeds in America—but it is also one that fails every day. People are often tempted by this dream, and as often as not, it turns out to be just that—a dream. Abel is unlikely to accomplish the extraordinary unless he has extraordinary ability. And by definition, the extraordinary is, well, not ordinary.

Cain isn't a dreamer. You won't often find him taking chances of this kind. He is calculating by nature and tends to play it safe. He gravitates toward where power and money are concentrated in the here and now. Let others go out on a limb and take chances; he will exploit and take advantage of their success *after* they achieve it. He is unlikely to strike out on his own, but rather is content to play his game within the rules set by The Momentum of the Familiar. One of the most basic of these rules is: Never upset the company by pushing for changes in widely accepted practices, unless you control the company.

A PROPHET WITHOUT HONOR IN HIS OWN LAND

Cain isn't a prophet; Abel often is.

A prophet is someone who looks down the road, anticipates problems, and pushes for action to prevent the problems from arising or becoming unmanageable. It is an invaluable kind of ability in business and politics, and it is largely unrecognized and unrewarded.

CASE STUDY 11

Andy and Betty were two very high-ranking officials in an important federal cabinet department. They were young, successful, affluent, powerful, and much taken with themselves. As they saw it, they were "Masters of America." Jim was a consultant who worked with them.

One morning, Jim walked into Andy's office and found Andy and Betty convulsed with laughter.

"Have we got a story for you!" they told Jim.

It seems that one of their political enemies—the head of an agency within the department—was in a lot of trouble, and they were reveling in it. The FBI was investigating a possible major fraud under a contract issued by the agency, and one of the agency's employees had just given a sworn deposition that contradicted the party line being taken by the head of the agency.

The agency head had telephoned the employee and screamed at him: "Listen, you stupid son of a bitch, you don't know what you're talking about! Next time you talk to those agents, you better get your story straight! Or else!"

Andy and Betty could barely spit out the story as they gasped for breath. "What an idiot. He's in *so* much trouble, and it couldn't happen to a nicer guy."

They were so busy savoring the distress of their enemy that they didn't notice Jim turning pale.

"Don't you two understand what has happened here? Your enemy may have committed an obstruction of justice by pressuring one of his employees to change sworn testimony."

"So what?" replied Betty. "That's his problem."

Jim continued: "But it's now your problem, too. You know about it, and your enemy also happens to be your subordinate. He's under your control, yet you've done nothing to correct his possible illegality. Your inaction could be seen as approval, in which case, you are implicated in his wrongdoing. You have to act now to protect yourselves before someone finds out what's happened."

Andy and Betty both protested, somewhat feebly, that Jim was being "alarmist." But Jim forced the issue, and Andy and Betty soon issued a written order to the agency head, directing him to send a note to the employee apologizing for shouting at him, and making it clear to the employee that he was expected to tell the FBI the truth as he saw it.

Afterward, when Andy and Betty discussed the experience, they told themselves that Jim was just a "worrywart" who had overreacted.

Of course, afterward Andy and Betty could afford to dismiss Jim's insistence on corrective action. The employee never complained to the FBI. No reporter discovered the story and plastered their picture on the front page of the *Washington Post* under the headline, "Government Officials in Possible Obstruction of Justice." Andy and Betty did not have to pay thousands of dollars in legal bills to defend themselves from accusations. And, since there was no public scandal, they didn't have to worry about being forced out of their jobs.

Andy and Betty could rationalize away these threats because the threats remained forever theoretical.

The fact that all of this may have been avoided precisely because Jim was perceptive enough to anticipate possible consequences and determined enough to force Andy and Betty into taking corrective action can be ignored because none of it ever happened. To do otherwise would require Andy and Betty to recognize and confess their own misjudgment.

In these kinds of circumstances, Abel will always be a prophet without honor in his own job. Most people are focused on the short term, responding moment to moment, day to day, problem to problem, concentrating on one small task, then another. They rarely take time to think about the long-term picture or think through the implications of "what-if" scenarios. There is even an incentive to ignore Abel when he warns about possible dangers ahead and recommends solutions, because these solutions may require additional work, unfamiliar work, and, in the view of many of those who have to do it, needless work. It is usually only the dedicated and perceptive Abel who cares enough about the organization to think about the future, to act, and to take the risk of averting possible, even probable, but still theoretical problems.

Cain can even turn Abel's perceptiveness into a liability for Abel by characterizing Abel as a Jeremiah or Cassandra—a prophet of hypothetical doom and gloom that never materializes. Naturally it rarely materializes . . . because an Abel, by anticipating potential disaster, often helps prevent it from occurring.

But how can Abel ever prove that he deserves credit for something that never happened?

The answer is quite simple: He usually can't.

CAIN TO THE RESCUE

A corollary to A Prophet Is Without Honor in His Own Land is this:

> ◆ **YOU RECEIVE MORE CREDIT FOR MANAGING TROUBLE THAN FOR PREVENTING IT.**

Anyone who has ever been involved at a high level in a political campaign knows that a single gaffe or misjudgment can undo a million dollars worth of positive advertising. George Romney's presidential campaign collapsed in 1968 when he said that he had been "brainwashed" about the Vietnam War. What would it have been worth if an astute advisor had said to him beforehand, "Don't say that"? And if the advisor had given that admonition would the candidate have ever understood how important and valuable a piece of advice it was? Would the advisor ever have received credit commensurate with the value of his advice? Of course not.

Cain knows that it's better to let the candidate half destroy himself, then come to the rescue. This makes sense when you consider what happens in any crisis.

First, people feel directly threatened. They may lose their jobs, which means they lose their incomes. A crisis is often a question of economic survival.

Second, this immediate threat creates a highly charged and emotional climate. Fear, anger, jealousy, and other primitive, exceptionally powerful emotions hold sway.

Third, anyone who eliminates the threat, or who is perceived to eliminate it, is a hero.

Cain will see the personal opportunity in crisis and will try to take advantage of it by using all the tools at his disposal: blaming others for the crisis, making others feel that he is their ally against the threat, making certain that he is perceived as part of the solution (even if he doesn't come up with a single useful idea), avoiding taking a definite position (in case it turns out wrong), and taking as much credit as possible once the crisis has been resolved.

Meanwhile, Abel works to solve the problem.

* * *

CHAPTER 6

Keeping Score, Stealing Credit, Placing Blame

Cain not only conceals the truth about himself from himself, he also hides it from others. He knows that it would be dangerous to make his craving for power apparent to his fellow workers. As we've pointed out, Cain isn't obviously evil. A Cain may be quiet on the surface, but he keeps his mind's eye on the prize.

He understands that it is far easier to gain power if others are unaware of your goal. "Understands" as used here doesn't necessarily imply a conscious determination by Cain; even when Cain is lying to himself, he still instinctively avoids displaying conspicuous ambition.

Cain is a public Dr. Jekyll and private Mr. Hyde ("Hide" is probably more accurate). The "best" Cains work their ambition quietly, behind the scenes. They are like the magician who can steal your watch while shaking your hand and leave you wondering what happened and when.

THE GATEKEEPER

Cain's subtle maneuvering for power begins with his efforts to control access to information and people.

Aristotle Onassis said, "The secret of business is to know something that nobody else knows." In other words, knowledge is power. In any situation, it gives you a leg up in argument, and successful argument allows you to shape decisions to benefit yourself. Just as important, knowledge can prevent you from making mistakes; for example, advocating some course of action that your superiors oppose. What you don't know *can* hurt you.

In any organization, information is blood. Every day, data about markets, profitability, acquisitions, contracts—even personal gossip—and all other aspects of corporate life circulate throughout an enterprise. To the extent he can, Cain wants to gain access to this information for himself and deny it to everyone else. This elevates him in the eyes of others. And by keeping others in the dark, they become dependent on Cain as a valuable source for what's really happening in the office and to the business. Cain feels most secure when everyone else around him is feeling insecure.

Abel sees information as useful in helping him do his job; Cain sees it as a tool for making himself more powerful, maybe even indispensable. Cain almost always has more useful information at his disposal than Abel because Cain acts in a determined way to get hold of it. Abel is usually content with the information he's supposed to get, and lets it go at that.

The lower down the chain of command you go, the more likely it is that you have to rely on the rumor mill to find out what's going on. Cain knows the rumor mill is unreliable, because he uses it to export his own misleading, self-serving rumors. In a business environment, most people waste time by dwelling on the past. They spend time discussing, analyzing, gossiping about what has already happened and ignoring what's likely to happen next. Cain is more likely to be focused on what he wants out of the future.

Cain also knows that to successfully maneuver through a corporate hierarchy, you have to gain access to closely held information, inside information, information about what's going to happen, not information about what has already happened.

The purpose of Cain's information hunt is self-advancement and self-protection within a limited range. Cain is a realist; he isn't aiming to control decisions about mergers, acquisitions, and other major corporate actions. Any Cain in a position to effect such megadecisions has already reached the power summit. Cain's goal is very practical: gain information material to his self-interest, particularly information he can actually use for his own purposes.

For example, if Cain has an early warning that the corporation is planning to downsize its workforce, he can act to preserve his own job, if possible, or if not, he can at least begin looking for a new job before he faces competition from other laid-off employees and before any prospective employer is aware that he needs to find a job. (It is always better to be interviewing for new jobs when employers believe you already have one; you don't seem like damaged goods, and you can negotiate from a position of much greater strength.)

Access to people can be even more important than access to information, especially if you are in a position to control the access.

CASE STUDY 12

Emily had accepted the job of campaign manager, and her reputation preceded her. She was a no-nonsense, take-no-prisoners, utterly cynical political animal.

On one occasion in the past, she had deliberately fired a young campaign worker, leaking to the press that he was let go because he was "too extreme." The young man wasn't extreme at all; he was expendable and in no position to fight back. Emily's actions were carefully designed to make her candidate seem more "moderate." The fact that she might destroy the career of someone totally innocent was inconsequential.

Emily was both calculating and suspicious. She didn't fully trust even her own handpicked staff. In her first meeting with staffers, she announced the following:

"Anyone who says anything negative to the candidate about the candidate's performance or about how the campaign is going will be summarily fired. If you have any complaints or qualms, you must bring them to me. There are two reasons for this: First, candidates' egos are notoriously fragile. They need constant reassurance and pats on the back. Second, only a few of us are in a position to understand how any decision fits into the overall strategy of this campaign. What looks negative to you might well be part of a much grander plan, which you should not be undercutting by raising doubts in the candidate's mind or in anyone else's mind."

Of course, Emily's real reasons for issuing her orders are obvious: (1) She wanted to insulate the candidate from any criticism, direct or indirect, that might impeach Emily's judgment; and (2) She also wanted to ensure that she would be able to identify, and get rid of, anyone who second-guessed her leadership. By limiting and controlling those who had access to the candidate, Emily consolidated and preserved her power.

In the day-to-day workplace, Cain can control access to information in any number of ways: holding closed-door meetings from which he excludes selected people (especially potential rivals), establishing a system where important office memos must be routed through him, threatening to fire subordinates who mention certain matters.

For any Cain, gatekeeper is an ideal position of power. It allows him to influence the actions of his superiors by filtering information, deciding what should be let through and what not. When one of President Nixon's advisors would meet with him (so the story goes), he would determine what policy or action he believed should be implemented in a given circumstance. Then, he would present the President with three options: two of them extreme, dangerous, or just plain wrong. Needless to say, the President nearly always ended up choosing the third option, which was precisely the course of action that the presidential advisor wanted.

Cain isn't content to act merely as a passive screen. He gets a "power rush" from the contacts he makes with important people who are on the outside trying to get in. If these people are important and powerful enough, he doesn't want to screen them out; he probably couldn't even if he wanted to. Instead, he wants to bond with them in the hope that they might be useful to him in the future.

For ambitious Cain, gatekeeper is an extremely favorable position from which to deal with the rich and powerful. He's not a subordinate under their command. Instead, he is interacting with them as an equal, someone who can give them something (access) they want. If Cain handles it well, he may create a sense of future obligation toward himself. "You owe me one," may be a subtle or even not-so-subtle message attached to the "favor" Cain is performing.

THE SCOREKEEPER

As gatekeeper, Cain is in a position to also be scorekeeper, which allows him to wield two other weapons in his arsenal: stealing credit and assigning blame.

Stealing credit is an art form to Cain. In the simplest case, he may openly grab credit for ideas, initiatives, or work that rightfully belong to another.

CASE STUDY 13

Lisa and Leslie had been assigned a particularly demanding project with a rigid deadline. The job had required back-to-back seventy-hour workweeks, including weekends, but Lisa and Leslie welcomed the challenge because they believed that their hard work would be rewarded and would enhance their reputation.

From time to time, their supervisor had asked Vernon to lend them a hand, and he had put in about an hour a day helping out. Vernon was a man who worked hard at *looking* busy, all the while letting others do the real work.

47

Whenever he put in even a few minutes on Lisa and Leslie's project, he would make certain to walk down the hall, stick his head in the boss's office and say something to call attention to himself.

"We're making progress on that project."

"I'm going to take a short break. This project is killing me."

"Things look good. I think we're going to make the deadline."

On Wednesday of the third week, with the deadline set for nine that evening, Lisa and Leslie were working frantically to wrap everything up. Vernon spent a couple of afternoon hours working on the project. At 4:30 he went out to dinner, returning at 8:30 for the last half-hour before the deadline.

When Lisa and Leslie finished, exhausted but pleased, they headed home for a well-deserved night's rest. Vernon stayed behind, writing a memo that he e-mailed to Carlos, the department manager: "It was a bear of a job, but we finally got it done. It's 9 P.M., and I'm heading home now."

He signed the note "Vernon," not even mentioning Lisa and Leslie by name.

Note something interesting here, and something typical of Cain: He's made a stab at garnering credit without technically doing so. If no one but the department manager reads the memo, Vernon may receive more credit than he deserves; Lisa and Leslie may receive less. He figures it's a shot well worth taking, especially since there is a good chance that any superior sufficiently removed from a specific project might well be wrapped up in his own problems and might not pay close attention to who is actually doing the unglamorous work. All the manager wants is the final product, in his hands and on time.

Vernon's note is both accurate and straightforward. It was a tough, demanding job; it got done; it was 9 P.M.; they were all going home. He didn't overtly claim to have worked on the project full-time and didn't try to minimize the contributions of Lisa and Leslie. Everything is implied; important facts are omitted, not asserted. If Lisa, Leslie, or anyone else ever discovers his memo and challenges it, he can always respond as the wounded innocent, "Oh dear, I never meant it to be taken that way. I just thought Carlos would like to know the project was finished. I'm really, really sorry." The sad fact is that many Abels would accept his apologetic explanation.

In the actual case this incident is based on, when Lisa and Leslie learned about Vernon's note, they were furious. They fired off their own memo to the manager, accusing Vernon of trying to steal credit for their work and effort: "We read Vernon's e-mail to you, and we can't adequately express how angry we are. We want to make it clear that the two of us did 99 percent of the work on this project. Vernon did almost nothing. All he did was sneak back for the last half-hour of work. Then, he had the gall to send you a note where he deliberately gives the impression that he did everything, and we did nothing. Well, we did it all, and we want you to understand this fact. Signed: Lisa and Leslie (and not Vernon)."

Later, when the manager mentioned the note to Vernon and told him that Lisa and Leslie were extremely upset about it, Vernon shook his head sadly and said, "Honestly, some people. I'm really sorry about this. I just wanted to let you know what the situation was with the project. As manager, I thought you should be kept informed. I wasn't trying to steal credit. In the note, I said 'we' got it done, not 'I' got it done. And, after all, you knew that Lisa and Leslie were primarily responsible for this project. I just thought they looked so tired and stressed that they could use a hand at the end. I signed the note with my name only because I wrote it myself, not the three of us. As I said, I thought you'd like to know the status of everything, and they were so beat and so anxious to get home, I e-mailed you as a favor to them."

Who do you think came out of this looking better in the eyes of the manager?

Would it help if we added this fact: Lisa and Leslie had acquired a mild reputation as complainers?

Or this fact: The manager himself was under a lot of stress from his superiors?

Or this one: The manager was a man who tended to think that women "whined" too much and often saw discrimination and unfairness where there was none?

Keep in mind that not one of these three facts changes the truth of what happened: Vernon was a Cain who deliberately sent his note to create the impression that he contributed more than he actually did.

In the real-life case, Vernon came out smelling like a rose; Lisa and Leslie like day-old kielbasa.

Why?

Consider all this from the viewpoint of the manager.

First, Lisa and Leslie have created a management problem for him—an unpleasant case of hurt feelings and accusations. Most managers respond well to those offering solutions—who make their life easier, not more difficult.

Second, the tone of Lisa's and Leslie's note is shrill: "We did all the work."

Third, it makes accusations that can't really be proven: Vernon "sneaked" back to work; he "deliberately" tried to create a false impression.

Fourth, their note is petty: "Signed: Lisa and Leslie (and not Vernon)."

Fifth, put it in context of the additional information about the manager: He thinks women tend to whine; Lisa and Leslie are complainers; he's got problems of his own and doesn't need another one.

As for Vernon, well, he comes across as a considerate and conscientious guy.

Fact: He did say "we," not "I."

Fact: The manager did know that Lisa and Leslie were doing most of the work.

Fact: The manager did want to be informed about the completion of the project.

Fact: It would have been presumptuous for Vernon to have signed Lisa's and Leslie's name to a memo they had nothing to do with. (They might have complained about that, too.)

Fact: Lisa and Leslie were tired. Vernon let them go home and took care of informing the manager for them.

Conclusion: Vernon is a well-meaning team player.

Cain triumphed in this case because of a hasty and ill-considered response by the two Abels.

It would have been much more effective for Lisa and Leslie to have thought through the matter carefully. If they had analyzed it properly, they might have recognized that their central goal—receiving due credit for their efforts, while correcting any misapprehension about Vernon's contributions—could have been better achieved by a simple, factual communication to the manager, a communication that completely ignored Vernon's e-mail, treating it as if it didn't exist.

"Wanted to let you know that we got the project done on time. Had to work late Friday, but finished by 9 P.M. Vernon came in for the last half-hour to lend a hand. Lisa and Leslie."

No whining. No unproven allegations. No pettiness. No problem for the manager. No opportunity for Vernon to twist things. Yet the point is made, on the record.

We could change the facts of Lisa's and Leslie's case so that their original response would be more effective than what we describe here. For example, what if Lisa and Leslie weren't respected because they were seen as too "mousy" and afraid to speak up for themselves? Further, what if the manager knew that Vernon was prone to playing these kinds of games and disapproved of him? And even further, what if the manager was the kind of man who respected people who were aggressive and blunt? And so on. And so on.

The point is that when you are faced with Cain behavior, whatever the specific details, you should:

1. Think carefully before acting.
2. Identify exactly what you want to accomplish.
3. Take into account all of the relevant facts of the situation—Cain's strengths and liabilities, your own strengths and liabilities, timing, the perception of others, etc.
4. Be realistic about what you can accomplish in a particular case. Don't overreach.

Cain also steals credit by retroactive decisiveness. Once an idea, decision, action, or project proves successful and popular, he quickly moves to associate himself with it, trying to give the impression that he either originated it or, at least, supported it from the beginning. Over time, it becomes part of his reputation and one of his "war stories."

CASE STUDY 14

Allen was a management consultant. Early in his career he had been an executive assistant to the CEO of a Fortune 500 company and had gained a reputation for writing a memorable speech about the social responsibility of American corporations. The speech had been mentioned by the *New York Times, Time, CBS Evening News,* and other national newspapers and networks.

But the eloquent speech was actually written by the CEO's speechwriter, a young man hired by Allen. No matter. In Allen's view, his own name was on the article, and besides, who was it that had the good judgment and perception to spot and hire the talented speechwriter? Why, he, Allen, did.

How did Allen continue to get all the credit? By shrugging modestly and never correcting those who congratulated him about the speech. Allen firmly agreed with what the reporter said in the movie *The Man Who Shot Liberty Valence*: "When the legend becomes fact, print the legend."

For Allen, when perception became reality, perception *was* reality. Why bother to disturb it?

Allen was also quick to pick up the phone and take credit for opposing decisions he supported or for supporting decisions he opposed. At one time, he was assigned to screen key personnel decisions in the company. If someone he fought against was hired anyway, he would telephone the successful candidate and tell her, "Well, my friend, we got the job for you."

Assigning blame is the flip side of stealing credit. When things go wrong, Cain feels that it is imperative to: first, evade responsibility; and second, having evaded blame, attach it to someone else.

One way is to avoid risk in the first place. Cain acts slowly and cautiously because he calculates risk, reminding himself that if things go well, he can always take credit retroactively. His philosophy on this score can be summed up as:

♦ **ABILITY IS LESS IMPORTANT THAN DENIABILITY.**

Cain is also a master of linguistic vagueness—a human fog machine. Qualifying words (adjectives and adverbs) and limiting phrases are his favorite tools, especially those that imply that he has taken a stand without actually saying anything definite.

> *"For the most part, I agree with what you say." (If things*
> *go wrong, it's the lesser part that will prove important.)*

> *"I see what you mean." (But I'm not taking sides.)*

> *"Okay, go ahead. But be careful." (By definition, if you*
> *fail, you weren't careful.)*

A prerequisite to assigning blame is to implicate others beforehand, and Cain knows this very well. At best, Cain would like to get Abel openly committed to a specific position. If this isn't possible, he will try to establish at least some amount of responsibility on Abel's part, if only by "running the idea past him." Blame can never be traced back to Cain if he makes certain that others are involved in the decision-making. His rule-of-thumb is:

♦ *NEVER TAKE A CLEAR POSITION UNTIL THE OUTCOME IS CLEAR.*

. . .

CHAPTER 7

Cain's Itch to Be Rich

Some cultural critics are fond of saying that greed characterized the spirit of the 1980s. But doesn't it actually characterize the spirit of always?

"Greed is good" could easily be Cain's self-justifying mantra. Greed is a hunger that feeds on itself. It is insatiable. Many a deluded person believes that if only he had a million dollars, he would be happy and content. But for a truly avaricious person, greed is never satisfied. The greedy just want more, and more, and then more. And Cain is rapacious. Greed infects everything he does and infuses his view of the world. It consumes his soul and impels him to do unethical things to try to satisfy his voracious appetite.

Now, let's face it: Many of us are greedy in some ways and to some extent. Most of us would like to be richer; some of us would like to be famous; others would like to have a better job or more power. But in Abel, these desires are balanced by other qualities: consideration for others, a dose of self-sacrifice, and basic kindness.

In Cain, the offsetting qualities of human kindness are relatively weak or nonexistent. Cain is truly greedy in the narrowest sense of the word. No matter how much he has, he always wants more—more money, more status, more power, more of all the material and superficial rewards of the world. Cain wants what he wants, and he wants it now. For him, deferred gratification is a cruel and unusual punishment. He is all the more desperate for success because of his insecurity, his inner fear that others are worthier than he is. He suspects that in a fair contest with others, he would be a loser.

Cain is so strongly driven by greed that he has an implicit understanding of its power, not only over himself but over others. For him, greed is both a motivation and a method to accomplish his goals. He can use it "positively" by promising, implicitly or explicitly, to reward you for helping him advance his agenda, or he can use it "negatively" by threatening to deprive you of something valuable if you don't give him what he wants.

CASE STUDY 15

Frank had a high school education, but had never graduated from college. He had come up the hard way, working on the loading docks and in the mail room, learning on the job, eventually becoming one of the top-ranking executives in a small company.

Although his position was relatively safe, he still suffered from feelings of insecurity. These feelings had become more and more intense over the years as Frank grew older and as younger, better-educated workers replaced the "old guard."

Frank now found himself in charge of a working group of twenty-five relatively young, well-educated workers, many of whom held professional degrees. Ray, who held a position directly under Frank, was one of these "college types" (as Frank sometimes referred to them all), and he was everything Frank hated.

Ray had been born wealthy, attended an exclusive prep school, graduated from a prestigious Ivy League college, and fresh out of college, through "connections" (or so Frank believed), had managed to land a well-paying job at Frank's company.

Worst of all, Ray was a talented hard worker, who Frank viewed as future challenger for Frank's own job . . . when the company might decide to save a little money by forcing older workers "out to pasture" and replacing them with younger, less expensive ones. Every time he thought about Ray, Frank's extremely high blood pressure turned his face a bright cherry red.

Occasionally, Ray would take an extra-long lunch hour, sneaking up the back stairs and into his office before Frank could catch him absent. In fact, Frank knew what Ray was doing, and Ray knew that Frank knew.

For several months, the two of them played this cat-and-mouse game, both taking it lightly, both winking and smiling about it, both treating it as nothing serious.

One day, Frank saw Ray as he entered the back door after a long lunch, made a quip about it, and said nothing more. Frank waited in his office while other members of the working group returned from their own long lunches. When everyone was settled at their desks, Frank marched into Ray's office and began screaming at him in a voice that could be heard throughout the office:

"You aren't paid to take an hour and a half for lunch! You try this trick again, and you're going to be looking for a new job! You understand?"

Ray was understandably shocked, but if he had understood that Frank was a Cain, he might have anticipated something like this. Notice how calculating Frank was: He let Ray get away with long lunches for an extended period of time, "setting him up for the kill," so to speak. On the day of the explosion, Frank didn't pounce immediately; he waited until everyone was present before staging his contrived drama. This way, he could not only intimidate Ray, he could intimidate the entire group working under him. It was a technique for keeping them off balance and uncertain of their jobs—a way of controlling them through fear.

Most people fear financial loss, and Cain, as in the case above, often uses this against them. The fear is normal because most people spend whatever they earn, and they come to depend on a rising level of income. This makes an employee vulnerable to Cain and puts him at risk of Cain's power. Worse yet, it puts his family at risk. The employee may have a large mortgage he has to pay every month; he may have a monthly car payment or two to meet; he may have large credit card bills. The point is not that the employee spends too much money. He spends what he can afford, but he can afford it only so long as his income remains constant. Cain realizes this and is willing to use the leverage it gives him to frighten and coerce the employee into submission.

SURVIVAL RATIONALIZATION

Abel's "greed" (using the word here to refer to the normal self-interest most people feel) can sometimes lead Abel himself to behave in a less than noble way. It can influence Abel to do things he is more or less ashamed of, but which he justifies in his own mind as "a necessary evil" or "unavoidable."

CASE STUDY 16

At the beginning of his career, Charlie had been hired by Betty as one of the salesmen working under her management. Betty was taking a chance on Charlie because he had no experience either in sales or in the company's field of work. But she had a natural ability to spot talent and was confident that Charlie would learn quickly and do well.

And she was right. In fact, Charlie did so well that within two years, he was offered a manager's job equivalent to Betty's at another company. Charlie accepted the offer and, before he left, thanked Betty profusely for the opportunity she had given him and for her faith in him.

Betty missed Charlie, not only because he was one of her best workers, but because over time they had become social friends as well as coworkers. Their families would get together several times a year for dinner, a picnic, or a cookout. At Christmas, they exchanged presents. Betty even let Charlie use her vacation house free of charge for a week during the summer.

A year or two passed, during which time Betty became tired and fed up with the hassles of middle management. She, herself, had risen from saleswoman to manager because of her own abilities, but she had been promoted into a job she disliked and found unsatisfying. Finally, Betty decided to return to sales and, in a reversal of roles, ended up at Charlie's company working for him.

Everything worked out well—for a while. Then, without warning, Charlie called her into his office and informed her that she was being laid off . . . immediately. Charlie told her that the layoff had nothing to do with the quality of her work. The company had run into financial trouble and was being forced to cut back. In order to meet his budget-reduction goal, he was forced to lay off the higher paid employees, of which Betty was one.

Betty was in shock. There had been no warning of an impending cutback.

"How long have you known about this?" she asked.

Charlie looked sheepish as he answered, "Three months."

Betty's voice was shaking, and accusatory. "Why on earth didn't you warn me? I could have been looking for another job while I still had one. You know that's the best way for anyone to approach another company . . . from a position of strength."

Charlie was almost pleading: "I couldn't. I wanted to, but I just couldn't. They said that anyone who told about the layoffs would be fired. I tried to warn you indirectly, as best I could."

Thinking back, Betty realized that Charlie *had* tried to warn her, if only with vague hints:

"The company's having some financial trouble."

"Who knows how long any of us will be here?"

"I'm not optimistic about where we're headed."

He had deliberately not deducted any vacation days or sick time from her record, even though she had taken several days off to take care of personal affairs. At the time, he had told her, "Forget about reporting them. You may need them later." It was a way of giving her a few extra days of severance pay.

From Charlie's standpoint, he had done what he could to warn and protect her. From Betty's standpoint, she was still out of work, laid off by a so-called "friend" who failed to protect her, a "friend" who was in the position he held only because she had given him a chance when no one else would.

It is easy, but perhaps a little unfair, to harshly condemn Charlie in this case. Granted, he protected his self-interest at the expense of Betty's self-interest, but at least he tried to warn her about the coming troubles and afforded her what little protection he could. After Betty's layoff, in the actual situation on which the above case study is based, Charlie went out of his way to send her whatever information came his way about other job opportunities, and he always gave her a superb recommendation when other companies checked her references.

The lesson of this case study is not that Abel is just as venal, ungrateful, and selfish as Cain; it is that Abel can be guided by self-interest (in other words, can, in a sense, be greedy) at the expense of others. He can be motivated to act against his higher instincts.

When Abel is trapped in this quandary, it is *survival rationalization* that allows him to live with himself. And, he has a point. Would Betty be better off if Charlie warned her? Yes. Would Charlie be better off if he were summarily fired for doing so? Would his wife and children be better off? No. Abel does what Cain would do in the same circumstances.

There is a difference, however. Abel doesn't use circumstances as a means of *deliberately* harming someone else; he does what he does because he sees no realistic alternative. Given that his hand is forced, Abel will try, as best he can, to help a person in trouble. It may not always be enough, but it is something, and it is very different from Cain, who wouldn't really worry about anyone else's problems.

FOOL'S GOLD

Not only can Abel's greed sometimes prompt him to violate his own principles, it can seduce him and warp his judgment.

CASE STUDY 17

Jack is an ex–Green Beret. In Vietnam, he had volunteered to drop behind enemy lines to observe and report on troop movements. It was one of the most dangerous jobs in the war, with a life expectancy of no more than a few weeks, but Jack was a born risk taker.

After the war, he formed his own contracting company and ended up making a small fortune. The money was nice, but for Jack the work was unexciting. What he really wanted to do was to make movies. He had enough money to independently fund a low-budget film, and he had an idea for a story, but he knew nothing about movie making—nothing about film budgets, script writing, directing, producing, or, for that matter, anything to do with the practical job of getting a film made. Still, he wanted to make a movie and was willing to risk a substantial part of his assets on the project.

Steve was a young attorney who handled the legal work for Jack's contracting company. He hated his job and, like Jack, had always wanted to be involved in the movie business. Steve had a small taste of "show business" when he appeared on camera as a consultant on the law for a local television station, and the television and film bug had bit him hard.

When Jack mentioned his idea about producing a movie, Steve jumped at the opportunity to get involved in the business. He volunteered to act as a middleman who would use the contacts he had made with television and film people to put together a creative team that could get the film made for Jack.

Jack met for a lunch conference with Steve and his team—a writer, director, and producer—to discuss the project. The writer, director, and producer were all young people and were willing to work for little pay in exchange for the opportunity to make, and gain credit for, a feature film. In exchange for guaranteed money up front, they instead would take a chance on the film's success and accept a percentage of the profits.

Everyone was enthusiastic about "making a movie." They talked excitedly about Jack's idea, and they all got along famously.

And the movie never got made.

The problem was the silent assumption each person was making about the percentage of profits he would receive.

As the man putting up the money and with the original idea for the story, Jack expected to keep at least 60 percent of the profits. The writer wanted at least 10 percent (he would turn a two-sentence idea into a ninety-minute story); the producer would settle for no less than 30 percent (without his practical experience, there could be no film); and the director wasn't going to work for less than 25 percent (after all, he was the creative force that would turn words on paper into an actual film).

Football players may promise to give a 110 percent effort, but when it comes to real money, 125 percent doesn't add up.

These five Abels forgot a simple fact: Twenty percent of something is infinitely more than any percent of nothing. Their greed deprived them of a chance to fulfill a dream, deprived them of an opportunity—perhaps a long shot, but an opportunity, nonetheless—to accomplish something that might have led to further opportunities doing what they most wanted to do in life. They were chasing fool's gold.

Con men know that there is greed even in the best of us. They depend on it. Any confidence scheme depends on the greed of its victim, on a person's willingness to be deluded by the prospect of easy money, easy fame, easy success of any kind. It is the weakness in each of us that allows con men to bewitch our better judgment. Not long ago, some people, more than a few of them wealthy and supposedly sophisticated investors, lost their money when they invested in a scheme that "guaranteed" them a return of 100 percent per *week*. In other words, it guaranteed that they would *double* their money every seven days. If you started off by investing two dollars, then over the course of fifty-two weeks—one year—you were "guaranteed" a return of two to the fifty-second power. After forty weeks, your two dollars would have turned into more than a *trillion* dollars, and you would be the richest man on earth. After a year, you would be worth more than the combined economies of every country in the world. Compared to you, Bill Gates would be poor.

How could "sophisticated" investors buy into this nonsense? Greed. They, too, were chasing fool's gold.

CAIN, THE RETAILER

Whenever gold was discovered in the old west, thousands of prospectors would flock to boom towns seeking their fortunes. Most of them never discovered anything and ended up broke. More often than not, the men who did best weren't the gold seekers; they were the retailers who opened saloons, hotels, general stores, and retail establishments of all kinds. The retailers knew that, rich or poor, people still needed and would pay for food, clothing, shelter, and entertainment.

Earlier in this chapter we talked about how Cain uses an employee's fear of losing something valuable to threaten and control him. But Cain can exploit someone's greed in other ways. Like the retailers of the old west, he knows what people want or need, and he will cater to these wants and needs in order to get something in return. He supplies rewards for supporting him; if not actual rewards, then the promise of rewards.

Sometimes the promises are direct, sometimes indirect. But overt or implied, they have one thing in common: Cain's promises are not guarantees. As Gertrude Stein once said about Toledo, Ohio, "There's no there there." For Cain, words and promises are instruments used to operate on other people. They have no intrinsic meaning to him; they exist only to serve and further his purposes, an attitude shamelessly expressed by Humpty Dumpty in *Through the Looking Glass:*

> "When I use a word," Humpty Dumpty said, in rather a scornful tone, "it means just what I choose it to mean—neither more nor less."
> "The question is," said Alice, "whether you can make words mean so many different things."
> "The question is," said Humpty Dumpty, "which is to be master—that's all."

Cain is the master of his promises; they mean exactly what he chooses them to mean, which is pretty much nothing. Abel is likely to accept Cain's promises at face value, at least until Abel learns from hard experience that Cain rarely delivers what he promises. In part, Abel's willingness to accept Cain's word results from the greed within himself; Abel *wants* to believe that Cain will give him something valuable in return for what Abel gives to Cain, just like the sophisticated investors wanted to believe that they could double their money every week.

CAIN'S STOCK-IN-TRADE

If Cain is a retailer, what does he retail?

As we just said, one of the things Cain retails is empty promises . . . but promises of what? The answer is: promises of anything valuable to Abel, anything that will convince Abel to do what Cain wants him to do.

Material wealth is the most obvious incentive that motivates human behavior. But people can be greedy for many other things: fame, awards, flattery, credit, even praise. One of Cain's innate talents is a knack for sizing up the particular weakness of an Abel. If Abel's weakness is money, he might promise Abel that he'll try to help him get a raise; if Abel's weakness is awards, he might promise to nominate Abel for one; if Abel's weakness is getting credit for his work, he will give Abel plenty of it . . . in exchange for Abel giving him something Cain values in return. Keep in mind that Cain is extremely focused and calculating: what he asks for in return will always be far more valuable than what he gives Abel.

SELF-INTEREST VERSUS GREED

Greed shouldn't be confused with self-interest. In the case where Charlie failed to warn Betty about her upcoming layoff, we said that Charlie acted out of greed "in a sense." But as we also pointed out, this isn't at all the same as Cain's greed, which is more akin to lust than mere self-interest.

Self-interest can have many positive effects. It is what drives a free market economy, where individuals pursuing success achieve it by providing for the wants and needs of others. They don't produce goods or provide services out of the kindness of their hearts; they provide them to make a profit and a living. But the end result is the same: They satisfy the desires of others. On a personal level, most people work out of self-interest—to earn money not only for themselves, but for their families.

Cain's definition of "self-interest" is both quantitatively and qualitatively different than this. He is so narrowly focused on himself that self-interest becomes greed. If he can advance himself by hurting someone else, he will. If he can only get ahead by breaking the law, he will.

Someone who's selfish will tend to associate with selfish people. There's a rule in real estate: "Don't buy the house; buy the neighborhood." If you invest in Cain, you are also buying into his allies, usually kindred spirits in venality. You may not think that his friends will affect your organization's "property values," but their malevolent influence is almost always felt, if only indirectly, by encouraging Cain in his greed.

In the end, Abel can't bring himself to act like Cain because Abel has to live with himself. And the self he lives with is kinder, more considerate, and more ethical than Cain's self. Abel knows that you can't take it with you, but along with material possessions, you do leave a reputation and a legacy behind.

2

• • •

HOW TO SPOT
CAIN'S CONS

* * *

CHAPTER 8

Cain's Spoken Agenda

We now begin Part Two of this book: *How to Spot Cain's Cons.*

- In Chapter Eight, we reveal how Cain uses the *spoken* word to manipulate people.
- In Chapter Nine, we reveal how Cain uses *writing* to advance his personal agenda.
- In Chapter Ten, we show how Cain projects an *image* to impress or intimidate people.

To kick off our analysis of Cain's *spoken* agenda, it is useful to describe Cain's attitude about language. Consciously or subconsciously, Cain uses language to manipulate people, presenting a stark contrast to Abel.

ABEL VALUES LANGUAGE FOR	CAIN VALUES LANGUAGE FOR
communicating his ideas	getting his way
persuading	manipulating

ABEL VALUES LANGUAGE FOR	CAIN VALUES LANGUAGE FOR
facts	flattery
logic	imagery
appealing to higher aspirations	appealing to baser emotions
businesslike words	buzzwords
words that have meaning and sincerity	words that are elastic and slippery
words that are promises	words that suggest "intentions"
words that reflect one's conscience	words that reflect what is convenient
words that are tools for building	words that are weapons for winning

THE WIZARD OF "IS"

Look carefully at the list above. Abel uses language to clarify and convey meaning; Cain often uses it to obfuscate and mislead. President Clinton was acting Cain-like when, during his testimony under oath, he answered a question by saying, "That depends on what your definition of 'is' is." He certainly understood what his questioner meant by "is." He was using the inherent ambiguity of language as a weapon to protect himself.

Always keep in mind that language *is* inherently ambiguous. Lon Fuller was a great legal scholar who taught contract law at Harvard Law School. Whenever a student would argue that the language of a contract was "clear," Fuller would turn to the blackboard and write this sentence:

"Time flies like an arrow."

Then he would ask the student, "What does this sentence mean?"

The student would reply, "It means that time passes quickly."

"Is that the only meaning?" Fuller would continue.

"Yes, it's clear. It's the only possible meaning."

"I'm afraid you have overlooked at least three others," Fuller would point out. "It could be read to say that there is a species of flies known as Time Flies which fly in a straight line exactly the way an arrow flies through the air. Or, it could mean that the species known as Time Flies are attracted to arrows. Or, it could be read as a command, that is, you should time flies, say with a stopwatch, in the same way you would time the flight of an arrow."

Fuller's point was that even the most apparently simple and straightforward language can harbor ambiguities, a fact Cain implicitly understands and uses to his advantage.

THE FORKED TONGUE

One of Abel's most naive assumptions is that everyone means what he says. In business or politics, this is dangerous thinking, indeed. Cain assumes that people are not saying what they really mean (after all, he doesn't), and it's up to him to read between the lines.

Cain believes implicitly in the dicta that "Talk is cheap" and "Watch what people do, not what they say."

As wary as Abel may be of Cain, he cannot truly grasp the fact that Cain frequently does not mean what he says. To Abel, deceiving people seems like an involved, rather draining, effort. He can't imagine that anyone could do this effortlessly, continually, even playfully, which is why an Abel is so often suckered by Cain.

Madge was the secretary for Jason, the regional sales manager for a chain of hardware stores. She was unmarried and could barely scrape by on her meager salary.

She told Jason that because of her long commute (which was not only time-consuming, but costly), she was thinking about taking a job closer to home; an ideal position for her had become available. And it paid a little more money. Maybe, for once, she could afford some of the things she had been forced to do without.

Jason, who wanted Madge to stay on for his own convenience, told her not to worry—the company was opening a new store in her hometown in a matter of months, and she could transfer there. In fact, he would recommend her for store manager . . . at a substantial raise in pay.

Madge couldn't believe her luck. Things were definitely looking up in her life, and she spent occasional moments daydreaming about how she would spend her extra income. She could afford some of the things she yearned for: a nicer car, maybe, and an actual vacation, not just a day trip to the beach.

A few weeks later, Madge learned from a customer that the plan to open the new store had been shelved months earlier. When she asked Jason what the real story was, he said, "I've been told confidentially that it's back on." He graciously accepted Madge's apology for questioning him.

A while later, she asked Jason when the store would officially open. Quite casually, he replied, "A couple of years."

Madge was stunned. Jason couldn't understand why she was so upset, even when she told him that the other job, with more pay and minutes from her home, had been filled and was no longer available.

Worst of all, Madge later discovered that the plans to open a hardware store in her hometown were dead and had been all along. There were no more moments of daydreaming.

Jason couldn't understand Madge's anger because Jason, always saying whatever pleased or impressed the person he was talking to, often forgot his own stories. Deception was so ingrained in his character and behavior that when anyone challenged him, he was genuinely puzzled as to what they were talking about. They must have misunderstood what he actually said.

Not all Cains are routine liars, telling so many lies that they forget them from week to week. Some Cains are calculating liars. They use half-truths—a lie like the basketball thrown at the audience by the Harlem Globe Trotters, the one with the long rubber band attached to it—a lie that can be pulled back at the last moment.

When it comes to lying, Cains often share an odd idiosyncrasy: They prefix an approaching untruth with a word or phrase signaling that whatever follows is the inverse of what Cain really means.

Listen for the following:

WHEN CAIN SAYS	HE IS ACTUALLY SAYING
"Honestly"	I'm about to tell you a lie.
"Truthfully"	I'm about to tell you a lie.
"Candidly"	I'm about to tell you a lie.
"Frankly"	I'm about to tell you a lie.
"Confidentially"	I'm about to tell you a lie.
"What I really mean is"	I'm about to tell you a lie.

How meaningless can words be? To Cain, pretty meaningless. In some cases, the only innate meaning words have for Cain is in whether they help him win power, status, or wealth.

Carl, a moderate conservative, was a candidate for his party's nomination for the United States Senate. He was a successful businessman and was running for political office for ego reasons, not because he had any strong political philosophy. In Carl's mind, he "deserved" to be a senator; it was the next logical step in a career destined for the top.

Carl spent a small fortune wining and dining party activists—lobster dinners, sumptuous cookouts, free tickets to the local professional sports teams—in a bid to win their support at the upcoming party convention.

But shortly before the convention, he lost a straw poll among party activists, three to one.

It was a devastating blow. Carl huddled with his top advisors to figure out just what he should say about the poll. How could he justify staying in the race with numbers this bad?

Together, Carl and his advisors decided that since his opponent was a well-known liberal, his best hope was to draw a sharp distinction between the two of them by emphasizing Carl's more conservative positions. At least this would make Carl the spokesman for a significant constituency in his party and give him a rationale for continuing on as a "voice for the voiceless."

Carl marched confidently into a press conference, took the podium, and told the crowd of reporters that he was "a man of the left" and would campaign as the liberal's champion in the coming months.

The reporters and Carl's advisors are still trying to figure out what happened.

It's hard to understand behavior this bizarre. The most reasonable explanation for Carl's incongruous statement is that he was indifferent to what he was saying. Carl was a driven man, concerned only with getting elected. He desperately wanted the power and prestige of high public office. Ideas, principles, words—what he was saying—were all meaningless to him except insofar as they might help him win the election. What must have been going through his mind is that since his opponent was more liberal than he was, and since his opponent had won the straw poll, and since most of the reporters were probably liberal, well then, he should tell the media and the public what they wanted to hear. The fact that he had been running as a conservative and everyone knew it just wasn't relevant to him.

In August 1937, Albert Camus wrote in his diary, "Every time I hear a political speech or I read those of our leaders, I am horrified at having, for years, heard nothing which sounded human. It is always the same words telling the same lies. And the fact that men accept this, that the people's anger has not destroyed these hollow clowns, strikes me as proof that men attribute no importance to the way they are governed; that they gamble—yes, gamble—with a whole part of their life and their so-called vital interests."

Camus' all-inclusive condemnation might be a little broad, but it still rings true, not only about political rhetoric but also about the many new ways language is devalued in a mass culture: advertising, bureaucratese, legalese, sloganeering, politically correct euphemisms, TV tabloid talk, etc.

Cain thrives in such a world. When words are no longer meaningful, he is freer to lie, pretend, and plagiarize because the culture more willingly accepts the fact that people "don't really mean what they say." Few people still believe that "my word is my bond." (Could anyone say that today without eliciting smiles from his or her listeners?)

Lying is only one of the ways in which Cain abuses language. There are many others, three of which merit special attention: ridicule, jargon, and flattery.

RIDICULE

David Lloyd George, a Prime Minister of England, once said of an opponent: "He could not see a belt without hitting below it."

This pretty well sums up Cain's operating principle when dealing with people, where one of his favorite and most effective below-the-belt language weapons is ridicule.

Ridicule is cruel and demeaning, and even Abel resorts to it occasionally, perhaps in self-defense, perhaps when he gets fed up with someone. But for Abel, the operative word is "occasionally." For Cain, the operative principle is "as often as it is useful."

And ridicule is especially useful for defeating ideas which are strong on their merits or opponents who have strong qualifications. When ridicule is used effectively, opposing viewpoints have trouble being heard through the pandemonium of laughter and derision.

Rumormongering is a subclass of ridicule. It is particularly dangerous because it occurs in a secret world where the subject of the rumor is usually unaware of it and, therefore, unable to respond to it. Rumormongering is often a deadly weapon when used against Abel, who finds it hard to believe that anyone would deliberately spread false, malicious stories as part of some effort to advance himself. Because Abel cannot imagine it, he isn't alert to the danger and cannot act against it . . . and Cain gets away with it.

JARGONAUTS

In our increasingly specialized age, professionalism has spawned pseudo-professionalism. True professional jargon is understandable—it simplifies and speeds up communication by shorthand references. But among pseudo-professionals, words, phrases, and acronyms are coined to impress, obscure, and control. It is a jargon that complexifies the simple for no good reason.

Although we said that some jargon complexifies "for no good reason," this isn't strictly true. There is a reason for this kind of jargon: in a word, manipulation.

Jargon continues to spread throughout the business world, and if you work among jargonauts, you know this all too well. A jargonaut rarely explains in understandable terms how things work or how to go about achieving something specific. It's part of his survival instinct. Gobbledygook makes it more difficult for possible rivals to learn the jargonaut's job, and, often, makes it harder to learn just how simple that job really is.

Abel is irritated by unnecessary jargon; Cain respects and enjoys it. He learns to speak it fluently (a contradiction in terms?) because it is a useful tool for manipulation, and he always keeps in mind the basic jargonaut rules:

JARGON NOTS!

Clarity   No. Better to shed darkness on a subject.

Simplicity   No. Make things seem too complicated for mere mortals.

Honesty   No. Better to use euphemisms that mislead.

Humility   No. Better to flaunt impressive insider knowledge.

Originality   No. Better to hide behind group-think and group-rhetoric.

FLATTERY

In *The Prince,* Machiavelli emphasized the importance of flattery for personal advancement. Everyone likes to be flattered. It makes us feel good about ourselves. Often, when we say someone is "charming" we really mean that he is an adroit flatterer. We find him charming because he makes us feel intelligent, interesting, amusing, attractive, or, perhaps, even charming ourselves.

This is one likable fellow.

Not everyone is a good flatterer. The secret is that you must make people believe the flattery; that is, you must make the flatteree believe that you believe the flattery. Cain tends to be much better at this than Abel because Abel is basically honest and finds it difficult to say things with conviction if he doesn't believe what he's saying.

Machiavelli wrote about the effectiveness of flattery directed up a hierarchy. Successful executives like to be told how smart they are; most don't like to be told they are wrong—ever. Cain is always quick to flatter a superior who can reward him in any way, and never criticizes a superior unless it serves Cain's purposes and can be done safely. "Safely" means Cain can credibly deny making the criticism if his superior somehow learns about it.

THE SOUND OF SILENCE

It is also important for Cain to know when *not* to speak out—when to keep his mouth shut. The flip side of language as a weapon is silence as a weapon.

In a debate or meeting, Cain will usually let others take the lead. Let someone else advocate or oppose (unless the proposal threatens Cain immediately and directly). Cain wants to get a feel for "the lay of the land" before he commits himself. How do his superiors feel about it? What are the positives and negatives for him personally? How do they net out? Can he just wait it out and pick sides after the battle is over?

This is silence as a strategy, but Cain also uses it as a tactical weapon. He will sit in a meeting and say little, occasionally making cryptic comments meant to sound deep and meaningful. Mostly, he just nods as if he understands everything and agrees with everyone. Meanwhile, Abel is sharing his thoughts about any and all subjects where he feels he has something helpful to contribute, staking out positions, admitting openly if he doesn't understand something.

When the meeting is over, Abel will think through what he said, wondering what he might have added to clarify matters. Cain, too, will be thinking about what Abel said . . . and wondering how he can use it against him in the future.

◆ ◈ ◆

CHAPTER 9

Cain's Written Agenda

Cain is inherently cautious; he will try to persuade verbally, one on one, rather than in writing, because writing can make it all too clear that he lacks conviction and that he's maneuvering for wiggle room, trying to protect himself on all sides.

Writing is especially dangerous because it can reveal Cain as ignorant about some particular matter. A poorly reasoned, muddled, ungrammatical piece of writing would diminish Cain overall.

This is why Cain only writes wrongs, using writing as a tool to manipulate an agenda or create a history that serves his interests.

HERE COMES THE JUDGE

Justice may be blind, but when it comes to judging potential competitors, Cain, the judge, sees very clearly. Cain sits in judgment over Abel when, as Abel's superior, he is responsible for writing Abel's yearly performance review. This allows him to manipulate how others higher up in the company perceive Abel. Is Abel "executive material" or not? Is Abel the kind of person we want to promote?

In this situation, Cain is most dangerous when he diminishes Abel with subtlety and delicacy. A heavy-handed assault on Abel's abilities or work product would probably backfire. Cain's superiors might—probably would—recognize the attack for what it was . . . and too harsh and too unfair a review would invite a counterattack from Abel.

CASE STUDY 20

Throughout the company, Brian was viewed positively by managers and his fellow workers. He was young, talented, very bright . . . and threatening . . . at least to Ted, his boss. Their management styles were completely different. Ted was slow and methodical; Brian quick and instinctive. Ted was insistent about his views and stubborn; Brian was compromising, always seeking a reasonable solution where differences of opinion threatened to interfere with getting a job done. Ted was narrowly focused, able to handle only one idea or problem at a time; Brian could effectively juggle a half dozen challenges at once, and handle them well.

Each year, the company for which they worked required all managers to submit a written evaluation of their employees' strengths and weaknesses. Ted's performance review of Brian was always "fair." It noted Brian's high intelligence, creativity, and overall skills. Scattered among all the praise, however, were several comments suggesting that Brian had limited ambitions.

For example:

"I am not convinced that Brian really wants all the problems of being a manager. He seems content doing what he is now doing," and, "Brian does his job, and usually does it quite well, but he doesn't seem to make extra efforts outside his prescribed duties."

For two years, Brian treated his review lightly. He was gratified by the compliments and figured the remarks about his long-term ambitions were relatively unimportant.

The company permitted Brian to include in his file a written response to Ted's reviews, but Brian never bothered going through the trouble.

But after others were promoted ahead of him, and after Ted's third consecutive review questioning his ambition, Brian wrote a blistering reply. In it, he argued, "Ted knows very well that I want to become a manager. He may question my ability in certain areas, but there isn't the slightest doubt about my aspirations."

Brian didn't stop there. He went on to analyze the differences between Ted's approach to management and his own, citing numerous examples where he, Brian, had stepped in to smooth over problems created by Ted's confrontational style—examples where Brian had essentially functioned as a manager to get the job done.

"On one occasion," he wrote, "Ted and Craig [another manager] were so at loggerheads over some minor difference of opinion that they refused to speak to each other. Meanwhile, nothing was getting done. I had to act as mediator, convincing each of them to give a little so that we could move forward and get something done."

When Ted read Brian's refutation of his own review, he turned pale. He realized that it was a damaging indictment of both his evaluation of Brian and of his own job performance. Ted immediately offered to rewrite his performance review of Brian, excluding any questions about Brian's desire to become a manager . . . provided that Brian withdraw his response. Brian agreed, and they lived happily ever after.

Or did they?

Ted was certainly happy because he talked Brian out of submitting a statement that would have made Ted look bad. At the same time, there were still two performance reviews in Brian's file questioning his desire for promotion and advancement.

Brian made a serious mistake in agreeing to Ted's offer, and an even more serious mistake by not replying the very *first* time Ted filed a review raising doubts about his goals.

Every Abel should heed the lessons of this case study:

1. Never underestimate the importance of a written record or its effect on those who have some part to play in your career.
2. Don't overreact to honest and accurate criticism, but don't treat it casually, either.
3. Be alert to criticism, even if it is buried among praise, and if you believe it is unwarranted, take advantage of an opportunity to set the record straight.

SETTING THE AGENDA

One of the best ways to win an argument and get your way is to control the agenda for discussion.

In politics, for example, it is well understood that the first and usually most important battle is over the question, "What are we going to talk about?" Some issues naturally favor one political candidate or party over the other.

Medicare funding has been a good issue for Democrats because the public believes that as a rule Democrats are more likely to favor increased funding for the program while Republicans worry more about controlling its cost—and those most directly affected by Medicare funding are those currently receiving benefits. Few of them want their benefits reduced or costs increased. For these voters, Democrats have had more credibility on the Medicare question.

Crime has been a strong Republican issue because in dealing with the problem, Republicans tend to favor the kinds of solutions the public supports (tougher sentences, death penalty) while Democrats are seen as "liberals" who want to deal with the problem by spending more money aimed at the "root causes" of crime (poverty, poor education). Reducing poverty may be an effective policy over the long run, but the public wants something done now. On crime, Republicans have had more credibility.

If the candidates spent their time arguing about Medicare, the Democrat usually won the debate; if it was about crime, the Republican generally came out on top.

In business and other areas, it's no different: setting the agenda can decide the outcome.

If Cain is in a position to do so, he will create a written agenda that favors himself. Consider a typical business meeting: If Cain is preparing the agenda, he will take the following into account.

- Who should discuss what, and in what order?
- What options should be considered?
- What should be excluded from the discussion?
- What do I want decided at the end?

Cain may want to assign Abel the task of describing the problem; Abel becomes associated with the problem while Cain positions himself as the problem solver.

By controlling the options to be considered, Cain can present the overall subject of the meeting in ways that establish himself as an important expert or, even better, as a catalytic agent. He can frame the topic as smart versus dumb, right versus wrong, us versus them, or in any way that he judges best suits his purposes.

As the agenda setter, if the meeting gets off track and things aren't going his way, he has the power to say, "That's an important point, but let's stay with the agenda and get back to it later," thereby squelching an unwelcome idea, or at least tabling it. At a minimum, it gives him time to figure out how to react to an undesirable or unanticipated development.

By using all these tools at his disposal, he can frequently lead the meeting to the decision that he wanted all along.

Something Cain understands very well is that in most companies ideas are everywhere. Executives are bombarded with requests, complaints, proposals—a fog of words in which it is sometimes hard to distinguish one idea or possible course of action from another. By controlling the agenda, you can lead people where you want them to follow. You can separate your preferred course of action from the amorphous mass of ideas floating around the higher-ups, and you can command and shape the attention of these same higher-ups.

Of course, there's nothing wrong with putting things in writing. It is good business practice and forces you to think through and organize your thoughts. Abel uses writing for these purposes.

But Cain uses it to control the agenda in a very specific way; he uses it to get his own way. Cain wants corporate energy and resources devoted to those areas he knows most about, and, as a corollary, diverted away from areas where his talents and expertise are limited. By doing so, he increases the probability that power will flow his way, whether or not this is good for his employer.

To paraphrase a well-known saying, Cain knows that the pen can be mightier than the sword.

KEEP QUIET, PLEASE

Cain knows when to write and, just as important, when not to. He understands the "Cardinal Rule of the Media":

> *"If you give me six lines by the most honest man,*
> *I will find something in them to hang him."*
> —CARDINAL RICHELIEU

Knowing when not to "put it in writing" and when to keep your mouth shut can keep you out of a lot of trouble. Every criminal lawyer understands this, which is why they almost always instruct their clients to say absolutely nothing to the police. And many a person has found himself in serious trouble because he created a paper trail leading directly back to him.

It is instructive to examine the way Cain thinks when he's faced with the question of whether he should put something in writing or not.

- Could my words be used against me in argument?
- Who is going to be reading this?
- Might these words come back to haunt me in the future?
- Can I couch my position with enough caveats to protect me and still not seem to be straddling or wishy-washy?
- Will this provoke my enemies to try to undermine me in some way?
- Can I write this in such a way that my superiors are at least flattered, if not persuaded?
- Should I test this out first on a neutral or hostile party?
- Should I get someone to co-sign this—someone I can blame later if things blow up?
- Is it safer to stall and see if things change before putting this into print?
- How will my thoughts look if someone leaks them or circulates them?

Psychiatrists might call this kind of thinking "paranoid." The problem is, it often pays off, which is why so many well-adjusted, mentally healthy, trusting people are working for paranoid executives.

THE HISTORIAN

Winston Churchill once told Franklin Roosevelt, "History will be kind to us because I intend to write it."

And he did.

Cain also is intent on writing history. He knows that most people are occupied by the demands of the moment and, therefore, have muddled memories of events if the events are only indirectly related to their immediate responsibilities. This gives Cain an opportunity to create a written record favorable to himself. Because most people avoid writing, especially "unnecessary" writing, Cain is free to become company historian for any given dispute.

The two most common historical records created by Cain are the yes-and-no memo and the secret message.

In a yes-and-no memo, Cain will try to have it both ways. Often, he may offer his "opinions" in an analytical format: here's the positive, but of course, we have to watch out for the following negatives. If things go wrong, Cain can always demonstrate that he had reservations about the idea. If things go right, he accentuates the positive.

A secret message is a document that Cain creates without telling anyone else that it exists. It usually contains a warning about how something might misfire. When it does, Cain can casually mention that he sent out a memo cautioning against this risk, calculating that in this Age of Information people often discard memos without reading them, give them a quick reading at best, and almost never save every memo. So, who can challenge Cain's assertion about his early warning, especially when he can produce a copy from his computer, a copy automatically dated by the computer as created months before any question arose? If others overlooked it, ignored it, tossed it away, is that his fault?

THE GHOST WRITER

One of the more amusing Cain tactics is when he acts as a ghost writer. "Ghost writer" here means something quite different from its conventional usage.

CASE STUDY 21

Whenever Rick met with any senior executive at his firm, he brought along a notebook and pen. Every time an executive said something "important," Rick would scribble away in his notebook.

The executives carefully noted Rick's seriousness and were especially impressed with the fact that Rick was so taken by what they said that he wanted to record and save their "pearls of wisdom." In their opinion, anyone with such perception and judgment was a young man who could be trusted with important matters, a young man to keep an eye on.

Actually, Rick wasn't writing much of anything in his notebook. The mere pretense of writing things down was enough to serve his purposes. As we noted in the introduction, this case study isn't some fanciful concoction. The authors have watched several different Cains use this gimmick on many occasions with surprising success. Flattery, thy name is promotion.

◆ ◆ ◆

CHAPTER 10

The Power of Image;
Or, Cain's Con Artistry

As with written language and verbal language, Cain understands the value of symbolic language—the status symbols, hype, and imagery that can impress and persuade.

Cain knows that projecting the image of success not only convinces others that you're financially successful, it also convinces them that you are successful at what you do professionally. Why else would you be earning all that money?

All too often in the "real world," perception is reality . . . and hype shapes perception. Cain knows how useful this image making is in acquiring, extending, and preserving real power.

CASE STUDY 22

Pete was an Assistant Secretary of Commerce, a shrewd operator, who decided to leave government service and establish his own consulting business. It was time to make some real money.

He was a true charmer, a "good ol' boy" from Alabama who someone once described this way: "Every time Pete walks away from me, I feel good about him and better about myself . . . but I always check my back pocket."

Pete's first step in setting up his business, even before opening an office, was to rent a limousine, getting a discount rate because he agreed to hire the limo owner's son as a chauffeur.

He once explained to a friend: "In Washington, lots of people have an office; only a few have a chauffeured limo. It's efficient because parking is scarce. But, more important, it impresses people. In my experience, nothing impresses people more than a chauffeured car. Most rich, powerful people don't have one, so when you drive up in one, they think you must be something special. It sets you apart from the ordinary, makes them remember you, and convinces them you're successful. The rich and powerful love to be associated with success. And they'll pay higher fees for the privilege."

The former Assistant Secretary is now wealthier and more powerful than most of the people he once tried to impress, and he still attributes some of his success to "the limo."

To Abel, this use of status symbols seems phony, even silly. Are people really impressed, for example, if your office walls are covered with pictures autographed by famous people?

If not, why do so many powerful, successful people have signed pictures of famous people on their office walls? The answer is because it *does* shape the perceptions of others.

Cain understands that our real personalities and motives can be disguised by how we act on the surface, by what we wear and what we drive, by all of the nouns, adjectives, and adverbs of symbolic language. To Cain, this focus on the external is not affectation so much as outright acting. Let the world be dazzled by the glitz, blinded by the lie. All the world is a stage, so why shouldn't we "costume" ourselves for success?

Cain's instincts are confirmed by the unrelenting pressure in our culture to constantly improve our appearance in order to acquire our heart's desire. The advertised messages may sometimes be subliminal, but they are certainly not subtle.

- Dress for success.
- Manage your image.
- Look good, feel good.
- Buy a whole new look.
- Impress for sex.

STUDIED HUMILITY

According to traditional American mores, people of substance don't bother to project an image. They are who they are, period. Most of us find it charming when a millionaire drives a Saturn and buys his clothes at Sears.

Such calculated and self-conscious "dressing down" is meant to impress in its own way. The message may be, "I'm so wealthy, I don't have to impress anybody." Or perhaps, "I may be wealthy and successful, but inside I'm just a regular guy." Whatever the exact intent, the point is that calculated humility is as symbolically expressive as anything else.

Obviously, there are many popularly accepted ways to self-consciously or subconsciously present yourself so as to inspire confidence. Something as simple as wearing a business suit is symbolic language—a kind of uniform. And much like wearing a military uniform, wearing a suit conveys this message: "I accept and am willing to abide by the rules of our game."

THE WAY OF ALL FLASH

Cain uses appearance as an end in itself to fool people, as opposed to building positive and mutually productive relationships. This is Cain's game—the way of all flash. Cain isn't building relationships so much as creating, in the words of novelist Norman Mailer, advertisements for himself. A good example of how Cain uses imagery to convey prestige and power is featured in the book and movie *American Psycho*, in which ambitious stock brokers try to outdo each other in designing their business cards. These Cains want their cards to shout success. They believe that their own corporate status is reflected in the quality of the card stock, the color of the ink, and whether or not the lettering is embossed.

Cain holds out an image of himself, like a mask. He wishes to project an image, yes, but equally important, he wishes to hide behind this self-created image—to hide his real motives, his insecurities, and his ulterior designs.

Projecting an image can become an end in itself, corrupting the self. Image replaces self-esteem; the image becomes the self. In this case, Cain doesn't feel comfortable unless he has the best seat in the restaurant. He doesn't feel real if his name isn't in the newspaper. He begins to believe his own press releases. He "goes Hollywood."

PUBLIC RELATIONS

Now, a genuine con man (an oxymoron?) will carry "image" to a petit larceny extreme. He'll fabricate letters of reference from impressive people, forge college degrees, concoct job experience. Cain doesn't even consider it petty larceny. To him, it's just "doing business."

CASE STUDY 23

A columnist recalls "the old days" when she did celebrity interviews for a national magazine.

"I would decide which stories to do, on my own, but then have to deal with P.R. people to arrange for them. These were almost always positive profiles—not puff pieces exactly, but pretty close to it.

"I was surprised the first time a P.R. person called me right after one of these positive stories was published and thanked me for writing it. Later, I found out that my story was clipped by this press agent and sent to the celebrity as proof of what she was doing for the client.

"In other words, my good journalistic work was credited to P.R. people who had nothing to do with it other than scheduling an interview at my request!"

Simply defined, public relations is a systematic effort to create an image for success that in turn creates new opportunities for success. The idea is to make your name, service, or product "hot," and then, when you're hot, use it, trade on it, leverage it up. Some P.R. is aimed at publicizing genuine accomplishment, but much of it aims to exaggerate accomplishment—making majestic mountains out of molehills.

In other words, "public relations" is often just con artistry in one form or another: name dropping, image propping, table hopping, scandal shopping, celebrity slopping.

But, sadly, it works—not always, but enough to make P.R. a major growth industry. Naive Abel recognizes that public relations is an effective, legitimate business tool, but he doesn't appreciate how much it does for individuals as well in the internal and external politics of any enterprise.

Andy Warhol's prediction, "In the future everyone will be world-famous for fifteen minutes," is an acid comment on modern P.R. It not only belittles the idea of fame, it skewers the modern sensibility that pays attention to fame instead of accomplishment and more substantial and enduring qualities.

Increasingly, the real world is based on the unreal. "Hip" has become the acronym for **H**ype, **I**mage, **P**erception.

Hip is no longer "what's happenin'" in the counterculture, but rather the nouveau cunning of the counterfeit culture—a culture of self-promotion. Cain moves easily through this world, a con artist conning himself and usually many others. He knows that increasingly the perception of success is the essence of success, and thus success in shaping perception is the most important kind of success in the unreal real world.

THE (UN)REAL REAL WORLD

Let's take a tour of this world.

The Imperial Office

The equivalent of a sleek limousine is an opulent office; if you have one, you must be good.

There are expert office designers, of course, who know how to pick the right plush carpet, into which your feet should sink at least half an inch; a power desk, positioned in the room so that visitors can almost imagine a periscope above it, so omnipotent is the person who sets course for all others aboard the corporate vessel; an executive desk chair that elevates the occupant; and facing the desk, a chair for guests, suitably lowered a few inches to ensure that a visitor is looking up at his host, like some primal hominid staring at the monolith in the movie *2001: A Space Odyssey.*

CASE STUDY 24

An ornery, independent-minded salesman loved to torment one of the vice presidents in his company whenever he visited his office. The vice president was vain and pompous and acutely aware of his own status. The walls of his office were plastered with his gold-framed college degree, photographs of himself shaking hands with minor celebrities (none of whom had the faintest idea who this person holding his hand was), and plaques of various kinds. The array was meant to impress and intimidate, but it only bemused the salesman, who found it pretentious.

"I'd always move my chair to put it at an odd angle to his desk. This would really throw him off psychologically. He had the seating carefully arranged for power, got used to looking down from his throne at his subjects. This guy would practically beg me to put the chair back, but I'd just move it to an even more awkward place away from him. It's amazing how you can create cognitive dissonance in a supposedly powerful person just by moving a chair."

Office decor is critical in effecting a prestigious look. It's about more than status symbols. It's about impressing people with everything about you—personal relationships, the books you supposedly read, ethnically correct art, politically correct photos, costly antiques, sports success, exclusive memberships, family memorabilia—anything that might impress, even if it's just some oddity that prompts a story about something indirectly impressive. "I picked up that rock when I was at Angkor Wat. You know, the Khmer Rouge were crawling all over the place . . ."

Proximity to Power

The location of an office can be even more impressive than its design and accoutrements, and this is true whether corporate or governmental. Those offices closest to that of the chief executive officer are seen as having more access to, and thus more influence with, the CEO. In some companies, ambitious executives will sacrifice a higher salary in order to gain or keep a desired office. It's not unusual for a vice president of a major division to make less than a sales manager or marketing v.p. but have an office closer to the president.

Some offices might as well be in Siberia. One company had what became known as "the dump-truck office" located at the opposite end of the building from the president's. Whoever had that office was about to be dumped. Fired. Quite often, the dumpee ended up in that office after being moved down the office hierarchy from a good office to a mediocre one and finally to the fatal destination. A company employee recalls the time when, "I was talking with a middle manager who had just moved into that office, and suddenly in came two guys with dollies. 'Oh, I'm out of here!' the manager moaned. 'No,' said one of the moving guys, 'you're in the wrong office.' I'll never forget the look of relief on his face."

Proximity to power can involve things other than offices.

CASE STUDY 25

The Chief of Staff for a former president was known as a master of the power game, and he could find ways of projecting his power in even mundane ways.

For example, he determined the seating arrangements on Air Force One. The closer you were seated to him, the greater the prestige; the farther away, the more you were on the outs and had reason to worry about your job. Eventually, those who were moved farthest away would be kicked off the plane altogether (usually before takeoff).

From Air Force One, you might be demoted to traveling on the press plane; from the press plane to not traveling at all; after that, to a smaller office; if you still couldn't take the hint, you might be transferred out of Washington and assigned to a subordinate position in some regional government office, maybe in Boise, Idaho.

Many Abels might think, "How petty and superficial of that chief of staff!" But his tactic worked because of the reactions of the people around him. If they hadn't cared about sitting near him in the front of the plane or cared about the size and location of their office, he wouldn't have bothered with his tactics. Perhaps it tells us more about the hangers-on than it does about that chief of staff.

The fact is, most of us are extremely sensitive to minor slights in the workplace. It may be because these minor slights aren't really so minor after all. Most people are acutely aware of their position and standing in any hierarchy, and they are also acutely aware that small and seemingly insignificant slights may signal a demotion in status. A good rule of thumb is this: If you think you are being disrespected and demoted, you probably are.

Privileged Parking

The third concern of the unreal world, privileged parking affords proximity to power by proxy.

In most companies that have assigned parking, status is proportional to the nearness of the parking spot to the main building entrance. (Now and then, a new CEO may reverse that policy to win popular support from the rank-and-file employees.)

Privileged parking might also be a function of whether the names of executives, rather than impersonal numbers, are placed on assigned spaces.

It's always interesting when a top executive leaves a firm: Who is going to get the vacated parking space? At one company, when one of the top five executives was fired, the remaining executives decided not to replace him; his position was abolished. To reflect this new reality, the entire parking lot had to be rearranged to make it clear that there were no longer five monarchs; henceforth, there would be only four.

Titles

The prestige given to parking, vanity license plates, and other silly perks also shows itself at the highest levels of our government. Reporters often add an unofficial word to the title of a certain Congressional committee chairman. The chairman of the House Ways and Means Committee is never merely the chairmen of the House Ways and Means Committee—he is always the chairman of the **powerful** House Ways and Means Committee. Why? Because among other things, he's the man who assigns offices, parking spaces, and other perks to members of that august body.

The Lone Arranger

In the unreal-real world, "The Lone Arranger" is an important fellow. He has the power to make the logistical arrangements for who plays, who pays, and who stays.

The Lone Arranger might be a "nobody" in the corporate or political hierarchy, but Cain realizes how important it is to get in good with him: He can get you the right seat on the bus, the right room assignment at the hotel, and, if there are three limos picking people up at the airport, he can make sure you're in the first one. Cain wants the Lone Arranger to be in his debt, so Cain will find some way to do him a favor. Abel, however, wants and expects only fairness in the assignment process. Of course, Abel often ends up flying coach and sleeping in the room next to the railroad tracks.

Guilt by Association

In the unreal real world, Moses Ben Maimon's (Maimonides) phrase, "Charity's Golden Ladder," has been given an ironic twist. Oscar Wilde once observed, "Charity creates a multitude of sins." One sin Wilde himself might have appreciated is charity as an opportunity for socializing, dining, whining, and generally showing off. The charity is quite beside the point, of course. What matters is the culinary skills of the caterer, the table gifts, the famous or influential folks in attendance, and whether the event itself is trendy enough to be worth attending.

Trendiness is crucial. Powerful people have only so much time to devote to charitable events and are unlikely to favor unfashionable, obscure causes. Because Cain always wants to be near the movers and shakers of this world, he will pick and choose his "charitable" contributions and activities with care, following the most popular charitable events like a California surfer following the sun.

Abel is not into air kisses and hugs with strangers, but Cain knows that charity begins at home, i.e., helping himself by schmoozing, plotting, and gossiping at every opportunity.

Trinkets

Toys and other trinkets are everywhere in the unreal real world—a kind of continuous bribery going on among people who can help one another in their climb to the top. It's back-scratching as an art.

Many businesses try to impress clients by buying sky boxes at sporting events or by indulging favored recipients with similar freebies. None of this has anything to do with how effective a business is at serving a client's interests, but it often works.

What's amazing is how cheaply some people can be bought off.

In both politics and business, even cheap trinkets can impress if the beneficiary thinks they somehow signify being "in" with the insiders. In Washington, for example, men fasten their shirt sleeves with cufflinks bearing the presidential insignia, sign letters with presidential pens, light their cigars with presidential matchbooks—all handed out by the White House to supposedly close friends of the administration.

Cellular phones, car fax machines, and other high-tech devices are personal trinkets. To Cain, they not only add a little extra flash and flair, they say to others, "This man is so important that others need to reach him everywhere and at all times. He can't afford to be out of touch for an instant." Before wireless phones were so ubiquitous, there was a popular joke concerning the executive who was so excited by his new car phone that he immediately called a friend, who also had a car phone. The friend answered and said, "Listen, could you hold on a minute? My other phone is ringing." The joke has become reality. In the early nineties, one minor executive, a Cain, was always trailed to meetings by an assistant carrying a cell phone in its cradle along with extra battery packs. More recently, there is the phenomenon of the multi–cell phone executive. Perhaps you've seen an executive sitting in a meeting talking on *two* cell phones at the same time, a phone glued to each ear while he ostensibly paid close attention to what was being said at the meeting. The next step may be picture phones, then multiple picture phones, then 3-D picture phones, and then, who knows, maybe holographic projection. The only thing for certain is this: If a new technology conveys self-importance, Cain will try to be first in line to have it.

Abel, again, tends to frown at all this. The expensive trinkets are costly for the company, and the cheap pens and matchbooks are an affectation. But once more the question arises: If it's all so frivolous, why do so many individuals and businesses play the game . . . and why are so many people impressed and won over by it? The fact that people see status and power in such things indicates how unrealistic it is for Abel to believe that this is a world where people are judged solely by the merit of their ideas, the goodness of their character, the fruits of their labor, and the consequences of their good intentions.

In the unreal real world, looks matter and appearances can deceive . . . and Cain's way of all flash is often the way of the world.

By contrast, Abel is like Charlie Brown, the innocent in the Peanuts comic strip: "How can we lose when we're so sincere?"

. . .

CHAPTER 11

How to Know a Cain

In any good horror movie, when the door creaks open and the music becomes ominous, part of you doesn't want to see what's going to happen next. A primitive survival instinct warns you to flee the scene before something pounces. In the "real world," Abel may cringe from knowing the truth about Cain for much the same reason: because it's scary.

In a movie, the worst that can happen is that a frightening image leaps from the screen. In life, however, there are real consequences when you turn away from the truth. Cain wants to be feared because fear empowers him; it allows him to control others. Cain wants would-be rivals to be intimidated by him. He wants subordinates to be anxious if they aren't busy pleasing him or carrying out his dirty work.

It's one thing to recognize and understand your own fear; it's another thing to surrender to it. Don't be afraid to face the truth about Cain.

In that spirit, let's review some of the personality and character traits that identify a Cain.

YOU KNOW CAIN BY HIS LOVE OF LYING

Perhaps he once won your favor by lying for you, and then you learned the hard way that someone eager to lie *for* you is equally willing to lie *about* you. Perhaps you fell for a lie that sounded convincing because it was so detailed, and yet fell for another lie because it sounded so reassuringly bland. Perhaps you fell for a lie because you knew that at least half of it was true, and passed it on as a reliable rumor before learning that the other half was malicious and false.

In whatever painful way you learned the truth about Cain's lying, one trait above all reveals him to be an undeniable Cain: He enjoys lying so much that he lies even when it seemingly gains him nothing. He cultivates lying as an art form, as a form of self-entertainment as much as self-serving expediency.

For all of these reasons, Arthur Schopenhauer, a philosopher who influenced many psychologists, including Sigmund Freud, offered this advice: "If we suspect that a man is lying, we should pretend to believe him; for then he becomes bold and assured, lies more vigorously, and is unmasked."

YOU MIGHT KNOW CAIN BY HIS ANGER

Almost everyone gets angry now and then, sometimes for good reason; for example, when an injustice is committed. But the wrath of Cain can be revealing of his true nature because he is likely to express resentments that go far beyond anything to do with the issue at hand. When he loses control and flies into a rage of abuse, he's baring the ugly feelings that animate him. He may well apologize afterward—maybe he will be ordered to do so by a superior—but don't make the mistake of forgetting what he actually said, because no matter how crazy the torrent of words seemed at the time, Cain meant to say exactly what he spewed. As unbelievable as it may have seemed to you, that was the inner Cain, the hidden Cain. You might like to believe that no one could really be so spiteful. Believe it.

YOU KNOW CAIN BY THE PLEASURE HE TAKES IN CAUSING PAIN

Novelist Gore Vidal once wryly observed, "It is not enough to succeed. Others must fail." Cain believes this. He not only finds ego reinforcement by diminishing others, he takes pleasure in inflicting pain. Psychologists may infer that he's acting out of insecurity or some childhood trauma, but, whatever the case, you should realize that he is genuinely sadistic. Realizing this, you should be alert and self-protective when he's around.

YOU MIGHT IDENTIFY CAIN BY CIRCUMSTANTIAL EVIDENCE

We live in a time of advanced forensics where we half expect DNA or video proof of every crime. Cain benefits from a similar "Are you absolutely sure?" attitude in the workplace. Many Abels can't bring themselves to believe that someone can be as bad as Cain truly is, so they give him more than the benefit of the doubt: They give him the presumption of innocence, no matter how much evidence points to his guilt.

Henry David Thoreau pointed out, "Some circumstantial evidence is very strong, as when you find a trout in the milk." Don't be afraid to be "judgmental" if circumstantial evidence makes a case against Cain. You shouldn't indict someone or try to get him fired without just cause, but it is better to be a little suspicious than to be a blissfully ignorant victim. And remember, there's a lot of truth in the old French proverb, "He who profits from the crime is guilty of it."

KNOW THAT CAIN IS A CONFIDENCE MAN

As we have seen, Cain is a *con* artist—someone who exploits the trust of others. Cain dupes people by appealing to the *con*fidence they have in his schemes, and by *con*vincing them to confide in him. Often, he accomplishes his purposes by shaming people into opening up, making it a test of their confidence in him as a supposedly trustworthy friend. Of course, by the time they find out that he's not worthy of their confidence, it's too late. By then, Cain has the upper hand . . . and he has a whip in it.

KNOW THAT CAIN LOVES TO DO FAVORS

This might sound like an odd quality to include in a list of traits that identify a Cain. After all, doesn't everyone willingly do favors for friends, family, coworkers, and people in need?

Ah, but what about motive?

Cain is eager to do favors—especially when he has to "bend the rules" or "shade the truth" to do so—because it gives him leverage over people. He doesn't want to hear "Thank you." He wants to say, "You owe me." To Cain, these are the three sweetest words in the English language.

When Abel does someone a favor, he's reluctant to even call it a favor. "No big deal. Just doing my job," he might say with a shrug, or, "Forget it. You'd do the same for me." For Abel, a person's gratitude is reward enough. He doesn't want others to feel indebted, awkward, or humbled. Cain is just the opposite. He will try to turn any act of assistance into a "personal favor," even if it's just part of his job, precisely because he wants others to feel indebted to him.

YOU WILL KNOW CAIN IF YOU LISTEN TO YOUR CONSCIENCE

When you are wary of someone, when you hear warning bells go off inside your head or feel a tingle of shame, pay attention. "Listen to the little man inside you," Cosmo Kramer advised George Costanza in an episode of TV's *Seinfeld*. George was never on speaking terms with his "little man," so he continuously got into trouble.

This is often true for the rest of us. When temptation rears its pretty little head, it's easy to ignore our conscience and rationalize our behavior. Cain depends on this; he counts on people to be naive about his ambitions and naive about their *own*. But what can you depend on, if not your moral compass? If you fail to listen to your conscience when it warns you about Cain, you will be listening to it later when it painfully reminds you that you should have known better.

3

...

WHY ABEL IS
AT RISK

◆ ◆ ◆

CHAPTER 12

Ability Redefined;
Or, Being Right Can Be Wrong

We now move on to *Why Abel Is at Risk*.

- In this chapter, we explain how Abel falls prey to Cain's many tricks. Is Abel naive, or just too focused on doing his job to pay much attention to Cain's ploys?
- The next chapter examines Abel's "miseducation." He may have done well in school, but school did not prepare him for real-world competition with ruthless people.

Can Abel truly compete with the Cains of this world? To answer this question, we first have to consider what we mean by "ability."

In the 1960s, Laurence Peter authored *The Peter Principle*, his classic treatise in which he argued that everyone eventually rises to his or her level of incompetence.

His reasoning was relatively simple. People are given jobs; if they do well in their jobs, they are promoted to a higher level. If they do well at this new, higher level, they are again promoted. And so on, until they finally arrive in jobs where they perform incompetently. At this point, promotions cease, and people remain where they are, doing a poor job—and guaranteeing a high level of incompetence in business, government, everywhere—until they quit, retire, or die.

Incompetent people are rarely fired, he explained, because it is easier for their superiors to tolerate incompetence than it is to suffer the unpleasantries that inevitably arise whenever someone has to make a tough decision. Even Presidents of the United States, such as Richard Nixon, Ronald Reagan, and Bill Clinton were notoriously reluctant to fire anyone unless they clearly violated the law.

But Peter overlooked a key point: He failed to adequately define his terms, making a few passing observations about what "competence" really means but failing to fully explore the question. People may rise to a level of incompetence, but what is incompetence, and for that matter, what is competence?

The problem in answering this question is illustrated in the following:

CASE STUDY 26

A well-known political consultant, Rob, was hired by a political candidate. The candidate was an easygoing man, even easier to manipulate—in Rob's hard-eyed view, the perfect candidate, someone who could be shaped and molded and "influenced."

Rob's first goal in any campaign was to "purify" the staff and rebuild it with people of his choosing—longtime subordinates and allies. In college, he had majored in history and had been much impressed by how Josef Stalin consolidated all power in himself by constantly purging anyone who might be a rival for power. To Rob, the power to fire people created fear, and fear was a most useful management tool.

In his early meetings with the candidate, Rob argued that the people working for the candidate were incompetent. They needed to be replaced. Rob would bring aboard a new, more experienced group to invigorate the campaign, make it more efficient, and give it greater credibility.

The politician reluctantly agreed, and Rob soon had a staff made up of his own people, a staff whose loyalty ran to him, not to the candidate. This was Rob's first objective because it eliminated potential rivals for control, rivals who might take credit for success or who might criticize the consultant, rivals who might actually be better, more talented, and more effective at what they did than Rob was.

Rob was a snake; the old staff was rodent dinner.

Question: Did Rob and his people rise due to their competence? If so, what do we mean by "competence"?

The consultant in the case study is a true Cain. He suffers from a special kind of jealousy—what we will call Abilityphobia—an intense fear of competing with those who Cain believes might be more able than himself. In his eyes, ability is not an asset but a threat. The consultant, Cain, fears that if he has to compete purely on the basis of ability, he will lose out . . . and he well might.

WHAT IS ABILITY?

This is a good question, and a hard one to answer. Ability cannot be defined precisely, but when used here it refers to certain qualities of human character that people generally recognize as positive and useful, qualities that help someone earn and thus deserve true success. Among the most important of these are intelligence, creativity, knowledge, skill, and hard work.

But this is Abel's idea of ability, not Cain's. For each of these abilities, Cain has a devil's checkmate.

IF ABEL IS	CAIN IS
smart	shrewd
capable	cunning
knowledgeable about his job	knowledgeable about how to get ahead
skilled at doing his job	skilled at taking credit
hardworking for company	hardworking for personal advantage

The most noticeable difference in this side-by-side comparison of characteristics is that Cain is much more narrowly directed than Abel. Cain is focused on promoting Cain, using whatever skills he has at his disposal to get ahead, even if these skills aren't strictly related to ability as conceived by Abel.

Worse yet, Abel is often naive about the world around him. He is working hard, concentrating on performance, and expecting to be rewarded for a job well done. Cain is focused on the perception by his superiors that he has done a good job. After all, these superiors decide who should be rewarded and who not. While Abel does well for the company, Cain does well for himself.

This is the missing piece of the Peter Puzzle. In everyday life, competence often has more to do with Cain's vices than Abel's virtues. By this definition, competence is measured by successful advancement of self rather than by competent service to one's employer or to the public.

THE CONSEQUENCES OF BEING RIGHT

Underlying the Cain-Abel interaction is a cardinal truth about human relationships: Abel's ability is a fundamental threat to Cain's personal advancement and ultimate success, and Cain knows this all too well.

It is bad enough that Abel might be right in a given instance, but worse yet, Abel might be right at Cain's expense. If so, Abel will make a dedicated enemy by exposing Cain's ignorance.

CASE STUDY 27

A television executive with good connections in the government secured a three-million-dollar grant from a federal agency to produce a documentary about medical care, education, and other important institutions in the country of Tyrania. She was overwhelmed with excitement at the opportunity. It was a chance for her to establish her professional reputation. If the project was successful, it would set her up for the rest of her career; it would certainly open up other opportunities to do exactly what she wanted to do with the rest of her life—produce and direct major television programs.

One condition of the grant, however, was that she must convince a prestigious television network to coproduce the program.

She met with the Regional Broadcast Network (RBN) and made her pitch. She was positive, confident, and enthusiastic. After all, no one would pass up three million dollars and the chance to produce and air a unique and important television program.

Unfortunately for her, Abel attended the meeting.

In the discussion that followed, Abel pointed out that Tyrania was a dictatorship that tightly controlled news coverage of its internal affairs. What guarantee could the producer offer that the hospitals or schools that Tyrania permitted to be filmed would be typical and not scenes staged for propaganda—Potemkin villages?

The executive and some others who supported her tried to argue that despite these restrictions much could be learned about a country that until now had been totally cut off from the outside. A documentary could provide valuable insights about this isolated nation and be a first step in convincing Tyrania to be more flexible and accommodating both with foreigners and with its own citizens.

Abel, however, wasn't convinced by sheer speculation about "possible" benefits. He insistently pressed the executive and her allies for an assurance that the project could somehow gain access to the "real" Tyrania.

"What guarantees can you give us that we won't end up as mere propaganda tools of the Tyranian government? As journalists, we can't allow that to happen."

The executive could offer no such assurances because Tyrania had never allowed any outsider free access for news gathering and probably did not intend to make an exception in this case.

RBN was forced to reject the proposal because of its journalistic ethics.

What did Abel accomplish here? What are the consequences of this scenario?

One consequence is that Abel demonstrated perception, knowledge, and principle. Another is that the producer lost a three-million-dollar grant, the income that would have come to her from the grant, the prestige of producing an expensive network documentary, and the future opportunities that might have materialized because of this success. A third consequence is that RBN, Abel's employer, also lost three million dollars that would have paid for part of the network's overhead and given employment to many of the network's employees.

Is this Abel's formula for success?

Abel's mistake is in assuming that people are motivated solely by logic, reason, and principle. He has failed to understand that if in being right you reveal ignorance or dishonesty in someone else, or if in being right you deprive another of something he or she desires, you have then made an enemy. If this enemy is a Cain, he will be out to get you.

This leads to a startling discovery by Abel:

◆ BEING RIGHT CAN BE WRONG.

In his innocence and gullibility, Abel normally assumes that being right is, well, right; that being right confers credit on himself and impresses others. Abel fails to ask the next question: Impresses them how? It might not "impress" them that Abel is tactful or a team player; instead, it might just give them the "impression" that Abel is difficult and argumentative.

In the case study was there any alternative for Abel; that is, any honorable alternative?

Of course, he could easily have gone along to get along. He could have jumped aboard and ridden the gravy train like everyone else. But for any Abel this is an unacceptable answer; it goes contrary to his ethical standards and his sense of pride. So, if not surrender, what?

One possibility is that Abel could have raised the key question, then allowed others to advance the discussion, perhaps offering an occasional comment whenever an important point was in danger of being overlooked. Instead, Abel took the lead in the discussion, hammered away at those on the other side, backed them into a corner, and left them no graceful exit. This may be an effective technique for winning a debate in the short term, but it is hardly a sensible way to win friends and influence people. In this situation, your opponents are less likely to remember and be impressed by your brilliance, honesty, and upstanding character than they are to remember that you embarrassed them and questioned their professional integrity in front of others.

A second possibility is that having identified the most serious challenge for those who believed in the project, Abel could have led the search for some acceptable solution to the problem. Very likely, there was none. But at least Abel would have come across as a more constructive and less offensive person, as someone who had raised legitimate concerns but who was open-minded enough to consider the views of others and possible answers to the questions he had posed. This should be a genuine effort by Abel to find a solution, not some artificial tactic meant to polish his image. (That's what Cain would do.) In fact, it would have been wiser in the first place for Abel to have followed the advice of the college professor who urged his students: "On first hearing any idea, resolve all questions and ambiguities in favor of the speaker; only then go back over the idea with a critical mind. If you begin by focusing on the flaws of anything, you tend to close your mind to its possible strengths."

Finally, Abel could have proposed putting off a final decision for a period of time. This would have allowed everyone to calm down, recover from the initial shock of Abel's argument, and reflect for a few days on the substance of the matter. During this cooling-off period, Abel could have patiently sought allies to support his position; he wouldn't be standing alone as the Great Contrarian, the Destroyer of Hopes and Ambitions. He could have gained allies by guiding rather than forcing them to the right conclusion. For example, rather than arguing vehemently for his own views, he could have asked simple questions one on one: "What do *you* think about this proposal? Can you figure out any way around the problems we would face?"

Since the vast majority of people are Abels, the vast majority want to do the right thing, but they much prefer figuring out for themselves the right thing to do; they resent being forced into the right conclusion.

Gentle, painstaking, subtle persuasion might be less satisfying than a dramatic, uncompromising stand on principle. It may seem less heroic . . . but as Will Rogers once observed, "Heroing is the shortest-lived profession there is."

WHERE CAIN'S TRICKS FAIL

For every principle there are exceptions that prove the rule ("prove" in this context having the slightly archaic sense of "test" the rule).

The first exception to the power of Cain's reach is at the extremes. There are a few Abels who are so brilliant, creative, knowledgeable, skilled, and capable that the arsenal of Cain's weapons are ineffective against them. Theoretical physicists didn't sit around arguing that Albert Einstein didn't know what he was talking about. And as humorist Tom Lehrer once said, "It is sobering to consider that when Mozart was my age, he had already been dead for a year." Mega-ability will almost always overwhelm any attempt by Cain to undercut it. So, any burgeoning Einstein or Mozart need not worry about the observations made here. However, if, like the authors, you haven't recently discovered a new theory of the universe or composed a musical masterpiece, you can ignore this exception.

At the opposite extreme, some Cains are so untalented that even scheming and maneuvering at their best, they still fail. And other Cains are so obvious and heavy-handed that their tactics inevitably backfire.

The second exception is that Cains lose effectiveness where clear and objective standards exist to measure success. The ability of a talk show host will be judged by ratings, audience demographics, and the sponsor revenue generated by the program. Critics may carp and Cains may plot all they wish, but if the host's ratings are high and the program is profitable, then by definition, the host is competent and has ability.

But, this second exception is limited in scope. Very few occupations, and thus very few people, are judged by such objective yardsticks. Most of us live and work in the vast mushy middle of life where rational judgments are affected by both emotions and perception and where Cain can easily manipulate the interaction of them. In this chaotic middle, normal expectations can be turned upside down; in some cases, competence (as usually understood) may not lead to success, and failure to get a job done can actually be rewarded.

If you are an Abel working with a Cain, the consequences of failing to understand your own vulnerability and Cain's hidden agenda can be calamitous. So read on.

◆ ◆ ◆

CHAPTER 13

Abel's Miseducation

Abel is someone who has an incomplete education. Throughout his formative years, until he enters the "real world," all of the most instructive institutions in his life combine in a well-intentioned way to give him a distorted view of the way the world actually works.

By words and action, Abel's family and the educational system tell him over and over again that good triumphs, that he himself is very, very special, and that if he does the right thing, he will be recognized and rewarded.

There is nothing wrong with this message. In fact, there is much right with it, and most of the time the lessons that Abel learns serve him well. But it is an imperfect message, one that in some circumstances leaves Abel with a provincial, childlike view of life, a view we might call:

◆ **ABEL'S FABLE: GOOD INEVITABLY WINS; BAD ALWAYS LOSES.**

(Keep in mind that "good" and "bad" as used here refer not to saints versus mass murderers, but rather to ordinary, civilized people working every day in conventional business, politics, government, or other institutions.)

Of course, as most adults eventually learn, this is utter nonsense. And if that's all it were—nonsense—it wouldn't be of much concern. But it is much more than nonsense; it is a distortion of reality that actually handicaps Abel in his battles with Cain.

So, what exactly creates this handicap?

FAMILY

Modern parents often dote on their children. They worry about them constantly, pat them on the back every time they do something well (or even not so well), place few demands on them, make every effort to stoke their self-esteem, and try to shield them from "reality"; understandably so, since reality as pictured on the six o'clock news is a Hobbesian world where life is "solitary, poor, nasty, brutish, and short."

Decade after decade, fewer demands are made on, and less work is asked of, the average child by his or her parents. Expectations are laughably low. It is a far cry from a century ago, when most teenagers never finished or even attended high school. Economic necessity drove them into the workforce at an early age, and they had to cope much earlier than today's college graduates, who can defer coping until their early, middle, or late twenties.

CASE STUDY 28

In 1907, Nicholas's great-grandfather, John immigrated to America from central Europe at age eighteen. He first worked the docks in New York—hard labor loading and unloading cargo—then moved to Chicago, where he landed a job in the stockyards slaughtering pigs. To many people, it might have been dirty, demeaning, low-paying work, but to John it was far better than anything he had left behind.

In 1917, John was sent back to Europe to fight with the American army in World War I. He returned safely, went back to work with livestock (or, in his case, deadstock), married, and had eight children, one of whom, Michael, was Nicholas's grandfather.

John died in 1933, in the middle of the Depression. Money was scarce, and Michael and his mother, brothers, and sisters were forced to live on corn on the cob for days at a time.

At the time of his father's death, Michael was fifteen and a sophomore in high school; he was also the only member of the family who had a job. He was forced to drop out of school and work full-time to support his family until 1941, when he was drafted and sent off to fight in World War II.

In 1942, Michael's son, Thomas, was born. Thomas not only graduated from high school, but went on to college, did well, went on to medical school, where he did even better, although Thomas did have to work full-time during his summer vacations and part-time while attending college and medical school to help pay for his education.

In 1977, Thomas begat Nicholas, who is now a sophomore at an exclusive private college. Nicholas was given a car at age sixteen and has worked only sporadically at part-time jobs. For him, both high school and college have been "party time." What money he earns is considered "his" money to spend as he wishes. His parents pay for his education, including a trip somewhere for spring break, because they feel it is their "duty." After all, they had him; he didn't ask to be born. When he finishes college, he may go on to graduate school, which he also expects his parents to fund, and which they probably will.

This case study is not only true, it is not uncommon. As we said, modern parents tend to shield their children from reality rather than give them cynical-sounding advice about the "real world." The prob-

lem is compounded by the fact that families today are better off financially and smaller than in the past, so parents are free to concentrate
their time and resources on fewer children. This concentrated afflu-
ence means that children face fewer demands and face them much later
in life than in the past (e.g., go to work, start supporting yourself, get
out in the world and make your own way). It is a much-delayed ado-
lescence, which is another word for naiveté, which is a prominent
characteristic of Abel's personality.

The upshot of all this is that when Abel finally is forced to leave his
family and go out into the world of business, he carries with him the
expectation that if he behaves correctly and does a good job, others
will give him praise, a smile, and a pat on the head. He is unprepared
for the indifference or even sneers that can greet his best, most successful efforts. Excessive family encouragement makes Abel feel good
about himself (and makes his parents feel good about themselves), but
it turns out to be very poor preparation for a sometimes cold, cruel
world made colder and crueler by Cain.

EDUCATION

The educational system reinforces the family's message to Abel by
throwing him a learning curve.

In the first place, schooling is based on "objective," measurable standards: test scores. Better students are rewarded because they do well,
which teaches them that if you do a good job, you will profit. Students
come to think life always works this way, that everywhere there is
some clear, objective, agreed-upon measure of ability and success. But,
as we have pointed out, it ain't necessarily so. In the political, business,
and institutional world, being right can be wrong.

What about bad students? Aren't they punished for their failure, and
don't they learn from this a tough lesson about how life really works?
Not in our modern educational climate, where teachers are expected
to encourage a squishy self-esteem among all their students. Johnny
may not be able to read, but at least we can make him feel good about
his ignorance.

For some people, education becomes a surrogate for achievement. They stay in school for long periods of time because it is a safe and affirming way of achieving without risking the hard conflicts of the outside world. (A point of clarification: We are talking about students and education, not about the faculty and the educational world. Most teachers, especially those who have been burned by academic politics, will recognize the lessons of this book all too well.)

By and large, schools do not prepare students for conflict, so Abel is emotionally unprepared for confrontation with Cain, let alone dealing tactically with him. It can be much safer remaining as long as possible within the academic cocoon.

Besides the traditional "three Rs," perhaps schools should add two more to the curriculum: reasoning and reality.

Schools are tolerably good at teaching objective knowledge and rational inference. But they don't do a very good job teaching creative reasoning. And they virtually ignore economic and political reality: understanding people, understanding competition, understanding strategy and tactics in dealing with people. What's going on isn't education; it is miseducation. Abel assumes incorrectly that he's being prepared for the real world, when he's really being prepared for passing a test . . . and little more.

It is important to balance the knowledge, rationality, and idealism schools teach with practical skills for surviving in the competitive arenas of life. Abel should think about Mark Twain's insight: "I never let my schooling interfere with my education."

CULTURE AND MEDIA

Mass culture and mass media are nearly synonymous these days. By mass culture, we mean television entertainment programs, movies, radio, the tabloid press, and pop music. Serious newspapers and magazines and serious news programs and documentaries are irrelevant here, since most people don't pay much attention to them.

In the past few decades, mass media has managed to sensationalize evil. Cheerleader moms who hire hitmen to kill their daughter's rival, skaters who hire hitmen to cripple their competitors, rich eccentrics who go off their nut and start shooting people at random, and other such aberrational loonies are the warp and woof of talk shows and movies of the week. If the measure of effectiveness is to prepare Abel for rivals who will hire incompetent villains to disable him (or worse), then culture and media are doing a good job in preparing him for what lies ahead. But if the measure of success is to prepare Abel for what he is likely to encounter, then culture and media have, in show business terms, laid a giant egg.

The day-to-day evil of Cain is subtle and mundane. What makes Cain effective is precisely that his modus operandi is not the outlandish, bizarre stuff that so enthralls movie producers and television programmers. Cain can manipulate Abel because family, education, culture, and media have given Abel little frame of reference to help him recognize, in Hannah Arendt's phrase, the "banality of evil."

The political correctness of modern mass media and culture also leaves Abel unprepared to deal with unfairness in the workplace. It may condition him to be "sensitive," but this also conditions him to half expect that everyone will recognize unfairness when it occurs and will act to punish and correct it. Cain isn't misled by any such sentimentality; he knows that if he does it right, really right, Abel will never realize (until it's too late) that he's been unfairly treated and, more important, neither will any of Cain or Abel's superiors.

Some may argue that the incessant negativity of news reporting actually helps temper Abel's gullibility. For example, the media has reported that most children cannot expect to enjoy as high a standard of living as their parents have, that nowadays it takes two salaries just to get by, and that a college education no longer guarantees a decent job, let alone a good-paying one. But the media rarely provides any kind of information that helps Abel deal with this reality. Moreover, it has nothing to do with Cain. In a peculiar way, Cain is an optimist who shrugs off this gloom.

Cain works on the assumption that his actions determine his destiny.

He takes control of a situation for his own benefit and often succeeds because of his focus and drive.

For Abel, the media's pessimism may be debilitating. It may simply discourage him from acting in his own best interests by sending him a glum message: "What's the use?"

4

• • •

UNDERSTANDING

CAIN

◆ ◆ ◆

CHAPTER 14

Psychoanalyzing Cain:
Three Perspectives

When we first began working on this book, we wanted to focus on the "real world" of ruthless competition rather than wrestle with psychological theories about personalities. But our curiosity got the best of us when we interviewed a lawyer who considered himself "an extreme Abel." The lawyer told us that his problems with Cains through the years had driven him to professional therapy and that his psychologist had been very effective in helping him learn how to cope with Cains.

This extreme Abel asked his therapist if he would be willing to discuss the Cain type with us, and the therapist consented. When we later reflected on what he said, we were struck by one salient thought: Cain was very real to him.

We were so intrigued by his comments that we called a friend who is a behavioral analyst. We wanted to find out whether another kind of therapist with a very different way of evaluating and counseling people also believed that Cain types truly existed. Despite his different interpretation of what shapes a Cain, he, too, saw Cain as all too real and very dangerous.

Finally, we contacted Ms. Norine Johnson, president of the American Psychological Association. She was intrigued by the premise of *Cain and Abel at Work*, and referred us to a psychologist with many years of experience dealing with Cains because this psychologist counsels people through bitterly contested divorces. He gave us a third perspective on Cain, and he, too, felt that learning how to deal with and protect yourself from Cains was vitally important.

Obviously, we could have continued interviewing therapists ad infinitum, gathering more and new interpretations of just what produces a Cain, but this would then be a book about various schools of psychology rather than a book of practical advice about how to identify and cope with Cains. Nonetheless, we decided to include these interviews because we believe that they contain intriguing and useful insights into an age-old question: How can anyone act this way?

The following excerpts are culled from our three interviews. We edited and reorganized the material to make ideas flow more logically, but these are the actual words of the therapists. We do not name them for two reasons: We don't want to imply that they are official or typical spokesmen for their professions, and we don't want their patients to wonder if patient-therapist confidentiality was in any way violated.

THE VIEWS OF A PSYCHOLOGIST

There is a continuum of personality patterns and development in human beings, and deviant behavior lies at one extreme of that continuum. Along the continuum, you find Cain near that extreme.

In the entire population of Cains, you're bound to find a large percentage of people who have personality disorders of one kind or another. Some are narcissistic, others are antisocial. Not every Cain fits this description, but most do.

Narcissists are excessively self-occupied. They are marked by grandiosity and a need to be admired, and they have an inflated sense of self-importance. They are intensely focused on self-aggrandizement. Antisocial types, sometimes called sociopaths, are willing to use others for their own advancement, and they willingly step on anyone in their way to get what they want. In interacting with other people, sociopaths have little or no regard for ethical and responsible behavior, and they feel no guilt about this. They don't see their behavior as manipulation; as they see it, this is just the way the world is.

Narcissists and sociopaths exhibit some of the same behaviors, but a narcis-

126

sist usually doesn't cause, or run into, quite so many difficulties as a sociopath does. Sociopaths are duplicitous; on the surface, they can be charming, and others are often taken in by this charm. But sociopaths have trouble maintaining relationships; their endeavors tend to fall apart, and they often encounter trouble with the law. They defeat themselves. Given that this is all a matter of degree, somebody who has sociopathic personality traits in excess might not be all that successful because a sociopath doesn't read social cues very well. A Cain is someone who has these traits to a lesser degree and is successful because he uses these traits as tools to get ahead in life.

Many public figures, especially in politics, have these personality characteristics but not to a self-destructive degree. To build a successful career in politics you must have a greater than usual degree of self-preoccupation, a much stronger ego than normal. This is almost a truism because politicians spend so much of their lives in pursuit of their own advancement. This is one reason they can survive public scandals; scandal doesn't make them dysfunctional because they have this potent self-esteem.

Many corporate leaders fall into the same category, as does any profession where you find an unusual accumulation of power. These people succeed because they are shrewd and skillful and share many of Cain's traits, although in them these traits are moderated and under control by the person—these types of people aren't so near the extreme end of the continuum. These are people who can form and keep relationships; they have meaningful attachments; they don't run away from problems, they don't lose jobs; they don't have major substance abuse problems; they don't keep shooting themselves in the foot. Unlike the more extreme Cains, the sick Cains, these people can function.

Most people are Abels. There is a tendency to think of them as naive because they are well intentioned, and they assume that everyone else is also well motivated . . . unless there is evidence to the contrary. But this isn't naiveté, it's normal. If someone has a positive view of life, he's justified in thinking that most people are like him. Obviously, they can be taken advantage of when they run into a Cain. Normal people can be fooled by Cain's superficial charm and surface attractiveness.

Remember Eddie Haskell from Leave It to Beaver? *He was always turning on the charm, trying to read other people, pretending to be sensitive. Eddie Haskell was exposed by the camera, but real characters are more subtle than*

Eddie. If someone comes across too much like Eddie Haskell, you should be suspicious. It's a cue to their personality. These are people who, by playing up their own accomplishments and projecting their most admirable qualities, can lure others into traps. One of their most admirable qualities is their ability to make you feel good about yourself; they are adept at flattery.

Cains have a polished manner. They know what is expected by other people, then they project exactly that. And they're good at it . . . precisely because they have no conscience. They don't care whether the image they are projecting is genuine. In fact, sincerity may be irrelevant to them because they are not even consciously aware that they're doing what they're doing. They don't really think much about other people at all; they are focused on themselves, on what they want, and they don't consider much of anything but that. When they do happen to think about other people, they see them as objects to be used for advancement. This is how Cain views the world, and how he views his place in it.

There is a temptation to say that Cains are produced by our current culture, which is driven by greed, but I don't know whether that's accurate or not. It may be true that in a culture given to material gain and the accumulation of wealth and possessions some of Cain's traits are more admired and encouraged than at other times. But I'm not sure that there's been any major shift in the personality traits of human beings. Any culture will bring out certain human traits, depending on the nature of the culture.

In a personal relationship, one warning sign that someone may be a Cain is the feeling that you're being left out of the equation too often, the feeling that something's missing, or the sense that events are being controlled to benefit the other person. If you get an uneasy feeling about someone—an impression that under the surface something's not quite right—well, that feeling is something you should pay attention to.

I see a lot of how Cains and Abels interact in personal relationships because I specialize in divorce. The traits that comprise a Cain are often the causes of a divorce in the first place.

For Cains, divorce is all about winning, because to them life is all about winning and losing. These are people who need to come out on top. Winning is a vital, important part of their lives, and they are more willing than most people to do whatever they have to do to defeat others. They will persevere as long as they must to win, and because of their perseverance they win more often than the average person. In a different context, their fierce perseverance is a trait that enables them to do well and succeed.

In many divorces I see men who are Cains married to women who either lack self-esteem to begin with or are beaten down by Cain during the course of the marriage. The wife is so dispirited that she is far too willing to give up everything just to get out of the marriage . . . just to get away from Cain. It's very common. Some of these Cains can outfight you, outwait you, and eventually wear you down.

I see this problem most often where a person with little self-esteem is involved in a divorce that takes a long time to resolve. They are left by the side of the road, suffering trauma and even abuse, their sense of self-worth further damaged, leaving them in no position to go after what may be rightfully theirs.

If you find yourself in a marriage where you are constantly feeling at the mercy of such a person, you should sit back and think carefully about your role in that marriage. Do some self-evaluation—and reevaluation of the marriage—and weigh the damage that this relationship is doing to your sense of self.

I said that for Cain divorce is all about winning, but I should qualify that. It depends on which Cain we are dealing with—the extreme Cain, or the Cain who isn't too far out on the personality continuum. For the less extreme Cain, if the relationship is close enough and meaningful enough, he may be willing to confront the problems in the relationship and listen to how the other person is feeling. But the more extreme Cain will never hear what the other person is saying. He may explode at the sheer nerve of anyone who dares criticize him.

The more extreme Cain is, the less likely he is to change.

The difficulty in dealing with these particular types of personality disorders is that a Cain isn't the type of person who stays in therapy. He's not very treatable. Therapy requires awareness of, and ownership of, your own problems, and this is difficult for a Cain to acknowledge. I would never say that there is no chance to save a relationship where an extreme Cain is involved, but it is a long process, and a Cain has little patience for it.

One of the most difficult kind of client for any lawyer is a Cain in a divorce situation. A self-centered, narcissistic Cain will expect a lawyer to treat him as *very, very special. One judge told me that the most difficult people to deal with in a courtroom are narcissistic, successful men; they are terribly demanding and will actually lecture the judge about why they deserve what they deserve.*

To a Cain, nothing is as important as Cain himself. Successful divorce settlements require accommodation, but Cains are unwilling to accept the slightest compromise. They truly believe their spouse deserves nothing, and they demand everything for themselves. Any demand by a spouse is evidence that the spouse doesn't appreciate Cain's worthiness.

These kinds of men marry women they can control. If the woman turns out to be stronger than Cain thought, then he abandons the marriage. A Cain is apt to become angry when he senses that his wife is becoming less appreciative of what in his own mind he has done for her. He will blow up at her nerve. "After all that I've done for you," is his typical reaction. Her failure to admire his worth devalues him. It taps into what underlies his personality disorder: insecurity, fragility.

Cain's disorder is rooted in a need to feel superior. His sense of self-worth depends on maintaining this feeling of superiority. When his wife grows stronger and starts making demands she hasn't made before, he may become more arrogant than ever, but underlying this arrogance might be feelings of humiliation and defeat. His solution is to leave the marriage and seek to reestablish with someone else the original connection he had with his wife, the kind of connection that makes him feel superior.

To successfully treat someone like this, you have to capture and expose his inner feelings. But a Cain is extremely unwilling to have these feelings laid bare. It is much easier for him to run away than stay in a marriage or therapy or anywhere that forces him to confront his narcissism.

I've been referring to Cain exclusively as "him" because these narcissistic and sociopathic personalities are predominantly male. But they aren't exclusively male. According to the Diagnostic and Statistical Manual of Mental Disorders, Fourth Edition, *put out by the American Psychiatric Association— for short, it's called* DSM4—*antisocial personality disorders occur in about 3 percent of men and 1 percent of women, a 3-to-1 ratio, male to female.*

Before I finish, I would like to reemphasize that human personalities fall along a continuum, and the characteristics I've been describing can be present in a person in combination with other, more positive characteristics. In many cases, *the final composite personality may serve a person well without necessarily being damaging to other people.*

Summary of This Psychologist's Views

- There are extreme personality types, two of which are (1) narcissists, who are self-absorbed; and (2) sociopaths, who have no conscience and use others for their own purposes.
- Cain has the personality traits of narcissists and sociopaths, but to a lesser degree, and he uses these traits to get ahead in life. To Cain, people are objects to be used.
- Cains are skillful at projecting an image of what people want and expect. They have a polished manner and are adept at flattery.
- To Cain, winning is *vital*. He will do whatever is necessary to defeat others. We can see this attitude clearly in divorce situations, where Cains will demand everything for themselves and refuse any compromise.
- Cain *needs* to feel superior for a sense of self-worth, and the more extreme a Cain is, the less likely he is to change.

THE VIEWS OF A BEHAVIORAL ANALYST

When I want to understand a person, I begin by asking the question, "Why is it that this person behaves in this way?"

From a behavioral analytic point of view, it is a truism that, in order to survive, any behavior has to be reinforced. Otherwise, it's not going to occur again. For example, people lie because they are looking for some kind of payoff. Whether or not there's a payoff—and the quality of the payoff—depends on the strategy they employ, which, in turn, determines the effectiveness of the lie. If it's a stupid strategy, a stupid lie, there will be no payoff. But if a person lies and discovers that he gets what he wants, there is a reward. It's survival of the fittest lie.

Throughout life, people are selectively reinforced. We learn from this selective reinforcement, and our actions are shaped into more and more effective behavior.

So, when we talk about a Cain, we're not talking about someone who comes to adulthood and suddenly, out of nowhere, begins behaving in an extreme, hateful way. If this behavior hadn't worked before and hadn't been reinforced, it wouldn't be there now.

How does Cain's behavior get reinforced? As a child I might do all sorts of things for M&Ms or a few colorful stickers. When I get older, I will behave in ways that elicit the kind of reinforcement that is important to me. To understand anyone, it's necessary to know what's important to him: wealth, status, social recognition, the smiles on the faces of people he serves. The exact kind of reinforcement that works varies from person to person because people like and value different things.

Some people are oriented toward social reinforcement; they want praise and approval from their peers. Now imagine you have someone who isn't reinforced at all by social approval; he doesn't care in the least what others think of him. If he only cares about what he wants, and cares nothing about the reaction of his peers to his behavior, what will stop him from lying, cheating, or even killing to get what he wants? The fear of getting caught and punished will stop him, but social disapproval won't. Yelling at him means nothing; refusing to be his friend doesn't make him feel bad. If he steals a client from a fellow salesman and the only consequence is losing the friendship of the other salesman, who cares? Social disapproval is not a reinforcer for a Cain. People who do bad things are motivated by things that are important to them. They keep their eyes on the prize.

Now, it's not easy to explain any individual's behavior. Most goals that motivate behavior are very complex and have all sorts of consequences. Some things have a quick payoff; some have long term consequences, good or bad. What motivates you depends on what's important to you.

In business, there's something called the Palmer Scale—how you answer a set of questions indicates certain things about your personality. For example, are you process oriented or task oriented? On the one hand, you get people who don't care if their group accomplishes an assigned task; they care if everyone contributes and is happy with the outcome. Task-oriented people care if they accomplish the task. How fast was it accomplished? Is the supervisor satisfied with their performance? For them, the reinforcer is getting the task done and done well. Most people are some combination of these personality characteris-

tics, although a person usually is oriented more in one way than the other. The point is that reinforcers are personal. They are different for different people.

Of course, nothing happens in a vacuum. We do things within a system. When he's at work, why does a used car salesman lie to his customers? Does he lie at home? At church? To his friends? Maybe he only lies at work. Why? Because that social system—the system that prevails in the world of used car sales—has some control over his behavior. The rules for that system are different than for some other social systems. The same is true for politicians; they lie only in certain situations. In the guise of national security, a world leader might lie to the citizens of the country he rules. Everyone will do bad things in certain settings. Ordinary, nonviolent people will kill in war, and a particular social system allows this. But we don't do bad things in all settings.

How do certain social situations encourage and allow bad behavior? Let's go back to used car salesmen. In a sense they are a brotherhood where each member supports the behavior of the other in order to help each other do whatever they do. They talk to one another in certain ways, for example, depersonalizing their customers as "suckers." They set up an elaborate environment which rationalizes their cynical behavior, and they adapt to this environment.

The Mafia is another brotherhood where immoral behavior is encouraged and justified. With criminals, the single most powerful predictor of recidivism is whether a criminal returns to his original environment. If they don't return, the recidivism rate is much lower than if they do.

Telemarketers are supported by a kind of booster club. Its motto is "Sell, Sell, Sell!" It doesn't matter if you lie; just sell, sell, sell. People enter this environment naive and end up doing things they could never have imagined. The operators take away their normal reinforcers. The only way to get reinforced in this environment is to engage in the behavior the operators prompt and reward. Everyone around you is doing it; in this setting, it's acceptable, even positive. Similar techniques are used to brainwash prisoners of war. The captors take away all your normal reinforcers, then they prompt you to confess and reinforce you if you do.

It's the same method a pimp uses to turn a young woman into a prostitute. He targets a girl who is much younger and much less experienced than he is, lavishes attention on her, isolates her from her friends, and builds a dependent relationship by controlling all her reinforcers. He takes her to a party, gets her drunk, and makes a suggestion: "Why don't you go to bed with my friend?

He'll give me some money. I need the money. Just do this one thing. It's no big deal." As soon as she does it, he showers her with praise, which reinforces the behavior. Now the girl is living in a new system.

In a school setting, the social leaders in any group dictate who is going to get reinforced, and for what. They set the tone. If a teenager doesn't drink, he may find himself isolated from former friends. For most teenagers, the social scene is the most important thing in their lives, so they have to go along with "acceptable" behavior in order to be reinforced as part of the "in" group. When you think about it from this perspective, there is nothing very different about the group of students from Columbine than any other group. These young men defined themselves in certain ways that gradually and inevitably ended in violence. Many groups could turn in that direction.

Ultimately, our environment, both personal and social, has a powerful effect on our behavior. Our history influences a lot of what happens to us. This presents us with a tough question: Is our behavior determined by exterior forces? In Beyond Freedom and Dignity B. F. Skinner argued that choice is illusory—we make the choices we do because we are built in certain ways. Our minds are affected by external stimuli, and we then behave in a certain way. We don't really "decide" how to behave; we just do.

In the biblical story of Cain and Abel, Cain was a completely free moral agent. His sacrifice to God was rejected, and he became jealous of his brother Abel when Abel's sacrifice was accepted by God. In his jealousy, Cain murdered Abel, but there was nothing that made him kill his brother. He was free to choose not to kill.

I believe each of us has the same freedom to choose our behavior. Our personal histories make us strong enough to predict the outcome of our choices. We usually know what the consequences of our choices will be, and we usually opt for the choice that will give us the strongest personal reinforcement.

So why do some people—Cains—engage in behaviors that the rest of us find outrageous? Because it works: A Cain gets reinforced by the success of his behaviors. These behaviors always have a tradeoff; some of the consequences are positive and some negative. But if all of the negatives are social (for example, "I won't be your friend anymore"), then a person who isn't socially oriented will have no inhibitions about behaving in an antisocial way. They aren't *punished when others dislike them or think badly of them. They simply don't care what you or I think of them.*

Many successful executives are Cains. They rise through a corporation because they are bottom-line people. Cains can make decisions without regard to how a decision is going to affect others. They get the job done by force, by ruling with an iron fist. They get the job done no matter what the consequences to employees, friends, or even their own families.

That's certainly the old style of management. But there's some evidence that the focus in business is shifting to management with a human face. Younger managers often look at older ones as out-of-touch dinosaurs who just don't get it. These younger managers have been rising because they care about people and can manage people as a team to accomplish an objective. Cooperation is in fashion. Where the old guard uses the threat of punishment to accomplish a task, the new guard uses positive reinforcement. Perhaps the new style of management is necessary with a better educated, more highly skilled workforce. Force may work when you are trying to get people to load more boxcars per hour; it's less likely to work when you're dealing with computer programmers or engineers, who in a prospering economy always have the option of telling you to get lost and taking another job.

Only time will tell which management style works best. Both punishment and reinforcement are powerful techniques, but from a behavioral point of view neither style will be successful by itself. My prediction is that we will come out somewhere in the middle.

Still, competition will always be with us. People's individual natures when combined with their histories of reinforcement can make people incredibly competitive—and people will do nearly anything under the guise of competition. Starting with a person already inclined to be competitive, Western society can produce some monsters. We take a basic human characteristic—competition—which is adaptive, important, and necessary for our progress and survival, and we pervert it into something that hurts both the individual and society.

Consider road rage. It is partly an outgrowth of competitiveness. Someone who is already stressed out and behind schedule is tossed into an inherently competitive arena. Who goes first? Who goes faster? Who gets off the ramp first? Who cuts off who? It's in-your-face competition that leads to negative behavior and negative consequences.

We have too many ants in the same anthill. By the end of the day, you wait to see who comes through it alive. Today, competition, in terms of survival of the species, characterizes our society more than most. Other societies may be a little more laid back, perhaps because they are less populated.

Hunter-gatherer societies weren't particularly competitive. It was only when work became specialized that society itself became specialized; that is, society became stratified. When society becomes stratified, then advancement up the scale is determined by competitiveness.

Competition is inherent in our democratic society, and it is a good thing, but if overly competitive people end up in the wrong position, then competition runs wild. If our behavior reinforces someone else along the road to reinforcing ourselves, then our behavior, even if competitive, is valuable to society. We may all be out for ourselves, but some of us are out for ourselves in a socially redeeming way. I give money to charity, and that reinforces me by making me feel good about myself because I'm doing the right thing. Maybe my gift erases some of my past sins or eases guilt feelings I have about the needy. But the point is that my giving also improves society. A sociopath like Cain doesn't care about that.

Summary of This Behavioral Analyst's Views

- To survive, a behavior has to be reinforced, and we are reinforced by what we value: power, wealth, status, social approval.
- Cain can harm others to advance himself because he doesn't care about social approval.
- Cain acts as he does because it *works*, i.e., it gives him what he values.
- Social systems can reinforce certain Cain-like behavior. For example, a salesman works in a system where selling is what's important, even if it sometimes means acting unethically (as defined by others).
- Although we live in a time when positive reinforcement often has replaced threat and punishment as a managerial technique, the fact is that competition will always be with us. Competition can be a good thing if, unlike Cain, we are "out for ourselves" in a so-

cially redeeming way (e.g., charitable acts make us feel better about ourselves).

THE VIEWS OF ANOTHER PSYCHOLOGIST

Sometimes I think professional people—doctors, lawyers, psychiatrists—are more apt to get sideswiped by a Cain. When bad things happen, professional people tend to think they should get involved, but if you are dealing with a truly bad character, you should stay away from him. An extreme Cain is beyond help.

As therapists, we are constantly asked to intervene in situations where we bring good intentions. When a child dies, someone has lost a husband or wife, or there's an affair going on, we're going to be there to help. Most professionals will treat anyone who walks into the office, even if they feel uncomfortable with the person. They don't do a character analysis of these people. They never ask themselves: Who is this person? What's his history?

There was a man referred to me for treatment. I asked him:

How did you get here?
Dr. X sent me.

Why are you here?
I've been fired from my job.

What was your job?
I'm a teacher.

Why were you fired?
I molested some kids.

Now, why was this man in my office? Was he feeling guilty about what he did? Did he want to be treated for his problem? No, he wanted me to classify his behavior as a disability because he wanted to sue the school system that fired him. He didn't want to be cured; he wanted money. I wanted nothing to do with him and told him to leave.

A physician may use the highest standard of care and professionalism in treating a patient, but if the patient is a real Cain, a really bad person, he may end up suing the doctor anyway. The physician may have no idea why this is happening. As a physician he believes strongly that it is his duty to treat anyone who comes to him for help. The physician will treat a Cain—who might well end up causing the doctor enormous suffering, might even destroy his career—because the physician has no ability to see the problems a Cain can and probably will cause him.

In The Road Less Traveled, *Scott Peck discusses evil, which is an out-of-fashion word these days. He says that no therapist should sit down alone with an evil person. It's not safe.*

Alice Miller looks at Hitler and evil in her book, For Your Own Good. *Her point is that there was a philosophy of childrearing in Germany at that time and in that place that produced a lot of people who were prone to Nazism. Today, if you look at movies of Hitler, he looks silly. But the Germans didn't see him that way. Their fathers were like that, and, in a sense, he was their father, the stern, forbidding father who set down the rules. If you disobeyed these rules, you were punished. Fear of punishment makes people feel powerless and weak. One way of coping with these feelings is to create a scapegoat. Now you can feel powerful and strong; compared to you, the scapegoat is powerless and weak and lives in constant fear of punishment.*

People are not aware of these feelings in themselves. They are in denial; they disassociate these feelings from their own childhood. They don't realize that their adult behavior is being driven by what they experienced as children. One reason they can do violent things to other people is because they have no self-awareness. We can't really help people who haven't come to grips with the idea of their own evil. There is no category for people who go beyond categorical thinking.

A Cain rationalizes his abusive behavior by comparing himself to the worst extremes of human behavior. A man ties his wife to a tree, cuts her heart out, and sticks it on a stake. Cain thinks to himself: I'm not so bad; all I did was slap my wife around a little bit. Focusing on the extreme makes Cain feel superior. I'm not bad; the other guy's bad. We split off that which is bad in ourselves and project it onto someone else, and they carry our sins.

I think there are people you just can't help because the damage they have experienced is so severe. As a therapist, I have no problem with this truth because truth is reality. If there's nothing I can do, then there's nothing I can do.

In cases of physical illness, we have no difficulty accepting defeat. We know that there are fatal illnesses, that there are times when, despite our great knowledge and best medical treatment, we know the patient is going to die. In these cases, the doctor says to himself, "I've done everything I can to treat this disease, but I can't change the disease process. I can't save this patient."

But when it comes to personality issues, we always think there is something we can do. However, there are extreme cases where, psychologically, people are incurable. They have the psychological equivalent of malignancies. I'm not talking about normal-range pathology. I'm talking about the truly extreme personality, something way beyond normal: a small percent of the population. Really malignant people have no conscience. They are so self-absorbed that they can't see how their actions affect anyone else.

Normal people can be obnoxious, difficult, or arrogant, but these people are not going to injure you. They have their troubles, and they may cause trouble, but they're not going to wreck your life. Truly malignant types—extreme Cains—prey on others.

There's no shortcut to figuring out these Cains. In the workplace, people aren't in a position to ask the right questions. They learn to spot these Cains only after experiencing damage at their hands. Unfortunately, as a wise man once said, experience is a bad teacher because it administers the punishment before it teaches the lesson.

These extreme Cains are motivated by revenge; they will do unto others what has been done to them in the past. This is one clue, in fact the only clue, to their character. In every case, evil people have had bad things done to them. Psychodynamically, they have been injured. They won't reveal this because they don't even know it. They have put away and denied their disturbing experiences. In their own minds, they have disassociated themselves from what happened to them.

If they have been physically or sexually abused, they will reenact that behavior in some way. They may become physical or sexual abusers themselves. Or they may use whatever power they have to hurt others. As children, they were powerless; someone did not respect their rights or feelings. When they grow up, they will have no respect for the rights and feelings of others.

Let's talk about people not being able to satisfy standards. A parent might set a standard and demand his child reach it. Regardless of how well the child does, it's never good enough. When this child becomes an adult, he will pass the experience on. He will make people feel that whatever they do, it's not enough.

Consider the case of a manager in charge of a corporation's annual report. He storms and rages about the look of a single page in the report and screams that the report isn't going into print until the page is fixed to his liking. He'll turn an entire group upside down over that one page, forcing everyone to work overtime, redoing the page again and again until he is satisfied.

Where does this behavior come from? As a child, he may have had a demanding father—a father who wanted him to learn to type. Maybe his father stuck him in a room and said, "You're staying in that room until you can type. When you can type a page for me, then you can come out of that room." As an adult, this executive reenacts his own powerlessness by imposing demands on those who work for him. Do it, do it now, and do it to my satisfaction, or you can't go out and play.

Many football coaches have this kind of fiercely demanding personality. Bill Parcells, the former coach of the New England Patriots, the New York Jets and New York Giants, once said, "This is not a job for well-adjusted people." He's probably right.

To understand a person, you have to understand what happened to him as a child.

I knew a clinical psychologist, the head of a mental health center. He got into a fight with a court clerk who had asked the center to service the local prison. The clerk argued, "We have emergencies all the time, prisoners who are psychotic and violent and need medication. You have to provide coverage."

The psychologist turned him down. "This is not our mandate," he said. "We are a community mental health center, not part of the criminal justice system."

The clerk asked, "Don't you have psychiatrists on staff?"

"Yes, we do, but they treat the patients here; they are not available to go to the prison."

The clerk was flabbergasted. "So, what are you doing in this town if you can't provide this kind of coverage? The doctor who served this community before you provided it."

They went back and forth until several judges got involved on the side of the clerk. Finally, the psychologist agreed to meet with the other side.

I sat in on the meeting as an observer. The judges and clerk kept asking, "Why can't you do this? It's your job. You're supposed to cover these people."

The psychologist kept insisting, "It's not our job. How many times do I have to tell you this?"

"But Doctor X used to do this. He came to the jail and took care of these people. Someone has to do it, and you're the only qualified people in town."

"Nope. Not our job."

I listened to this exchange for a while, then I asked the psychologist, "Was your father a physician?"

"Yes, he was."

"How old were you when he died?"

"Twelve."

With that, he burst into tears, and the meeting was over.

The clerk and the judges could have gone on for another six months or a year arguing about whether this man was going to provide coverage for the prison, and he was going to resist. Why? Because as a child he was abandoned by his father, who was supposed to care for him. Now he was abandoning those he himself was supposed to care for. The problem was compounded by the fact that his father was an authority figure, an authority figure the psychologist resented because of the abandonment. So when these other authority figures—the clerk and the judges—began making demands on the psychologist, especially demands about caring, he was bound to resist them.

People always bring their family to the office: Daddy's there, mommy's there, big brother's there. They project these influential figures on to other people or act out certain feelings they have about them. Mommy is either going to comfort them or not. Daddy is going to be strong, or daddy's going to be weak. Big brother is going to be in competition, or provide protection. Maybe they expect to be the center of attention. They externalize their family

141

experience and reenact this experience with others. That's why people are less productive at work than they could be. They are working through all these other issues.

I think we're in constant denial about where abusive behavior comes from. It comes from the family. People reenact past experiences. They do to others what was done to them. It might not be the parents who were abusive; it might be an older sibling or others in the family. Everyone has issues that underlie seemingly irrational behavior. I think 50 percent of cases where there is trouble occur because people are unaware of what they're reenacting. They don't understand themselves; if they did, it would be a big step forward in correcting their behavior. It's not a matter of forgiving themselves; it's just a matter of understanding what's really going on between you and others.

A bright person may use his intelligence as a weapon to degrade people, telling them, "You're stupid. You don't know what you're talking about." It's his way of avenging the psychic wounds he suffered in the past. But the wounds will never heal because the person denies and ignores the wounds, so they grow worse, all the while aggravating the person.

If people feel powerless when young, they don't ever want to feel that way again. They are terrified of feeling helpless. So, they become Cain, always seeking power. They internalize the person who abused them; they become that person. And that person identifies with the aggressor, not the victim. Their only other choice is to continue to be the victim.

In an office setting, the problems involve emotional abuse, and these are the kinds of cases I see in my practice. I see people who are tearing their hair out because they've been ridiculed, belittled, emotionally injured on the job. They end up not being able to compete effectively.

It's very, very hard for anyone to resolve these problems in the workplace itself. I've had patients who were highly enlightened and self-aware try to transfer and apply their insight to the workplace, but the people they work with will turn away from the problems. You can't communicate anything to people who refuse to hear what you are saying. You can't tell them that you represent their sister. You can't tell them that the reason the two of you can't work together is that you represent their father.

So, enlightenment doesn't help at all. Oh, it may help the individual understand what's happening, but it rarely changes what's happening. But at least understanding means you won't try to get revenge against the other person, which only perpetuates the cycle.

Revenge won't satisfy any inner need. Look at serial killers: How many people do they have to kill before they have exorcised their demons? One? Two? Ten? How many murders did Ted Bundy commit?

Even if you understand the motivation for someone's behavior—for example, an abusive boss—it's a mistake to think you can somehow "cure" him. You can't confront an abusive person about his problems; he'll only make your life more miserable. It's difficult to get around him by appealing to a higher authority, because most organizations are hierarchical, and the hierarchy resists violating its own structure. After all, if you can circumvent your boss, what's to prevent everyone from circumventing their bosses? And one of the bosses who might be circumvented is the very person you are appealing to.

It's better not to be around an abusive individual. I would choose to get right out of there. Of course, many people don't have that option. They may be trapped in the situation, trapped financially or in some other way.

It's not encouraging, but it's reality. The one positive thing is that if you understand what's really going on, you won't internalize it and blame yourself. At least you can say, "It's his problem, not mine." And if you can't solve the problem enough to live with it, then you have to ask yourself if you have options. Can you avoid this Cain at work? If not, are you in a position to quit and find another job? You might have no other choice, because if a person is genuinely abusive, his behavior isn't going to improve.

There is only one way for anyone to change, and that is to face up to what has happened to him and refuse to be either victim or victimizer. That's the right choice, the moral choice. Temperament is an important part of making the right choice—nature, not nurture. A person timid by nature may not be able to overcome his temperament and might remain a victim all his life. He can't escape from himself.

Anyone who has suffered trauma in childhood ends up on one side or the other: victim or victimizer. Trauma is anything that prevents a child from developing in a positive way, anything that denies a child what he or she needs to grow into a healthy adult. Trauma doesn't have to be abuse. It can be caused by failing to recognize and fulfill a child's needs.

There is an emotional side to life that we don't pay much attention to, not in families, not in school. But Cains pay attention to it. They know how to use psychology as a tool to control others because they learned at the foot of the master—they learned how to be hurtful and abusive from whoever did it to them.

Summary of This Psychologist's Views

- Adult behavior is driven by childhood experiences. A Cain is someone who has been damaged as a child and will now do to others what was done to him.
- If Cain was abused as a child, he will become an abusing adult. If made to feel powerless, he will seek power because he never wants to feel powerless again. If he had a demanding father, he will become a demanding adult.
- People reenact their past experience. Trouble arises when people do not understand and accept this fact about themselves. You have to accept this truth to have any hope of getting better.
- At work, Cain will resort to emotional abuse to control others. It is very difficult to solve this problem in the office itself. Most often, the only solution is to avoid the abusive person.
- In cases of physical illness, we accept the fact that sometimes an illness is incurable, but in a case of mental or emotional problems, we insist that there *must* be a cure. But Cain is beyond help because he doesn't *want* to be cured.

Although these three professionals look at Cain's personality from different perspectives, they clearly agree on some basic truths about him.

First, *Cain is an extreme personality.* He's not typical of most people; he's abnormal. Most normal people are Abels who care about others and are motivated by more than power, wealth, and status.

Second, *Cain is willing to hurt others to advance himself.* He wants to *win at all costs* and has very little concern or conscience about the harm he does others in his drive for success. Cain doesn't truly care what others think of him.

Third, *Cain is skillful at what he does*, and Abel is extremely vulnerable to Cain's abusive behavior.

Fourth, *it is very, very difficult to change a Cain*. You try to reform him at your own risk.

And that is pretty much what we've been trying to tell you all along.

5

...

HOW TO SURVIVE
IN A WORLD
FULL OF CAINS

. . .

CHAPTER 15

Why Cains Thrive

As we enter a new millennium, we hear countless forecasts from futurists about "our changing world." If we generalized about futurists half as much as they do about us, we might end up with this observation: Futurists are so focused on the macro they often fail to see micro indicators all around them; they see the forest, not the trees.

The forest is the "big picture": mass society, economy, culture, technology. The trees are the individual human attitudes and values that are shaped, defined, and redefined by the big picture, and which, in turn, shape, define, and redefine the big picture.

Futurists see "megatrends" in terms of data about tangible things (technology, demographics, etc.), but they often miss intangibles that are equally revealing, leading them to some awfully optimistic, but unrealistic, conclusions. For example, many futurists foresaw the globalization of the world economy as a trend, but their corollary assumption that we'd become citizens of a "global village" missed the mark. In recent years we've seen more of a "balkanization" of the world, with countries breaking up into warring ethnic factions, and factions splitting up into tribes. Who would have thought a generation ago that Quebec might secede from Canada, or that in the United

States the question of whether English should be considered our official language would become controversial and divisive?

Human nature and culture are not as predictable as economics, yet it is the changing personal and cultural values of society that are the true "leading indicators" of what our world will become. If we're to understand the nature of success in the changing "real world," we have to go beyond analyzing consumer data and economic trends. We have to understand real-world competition in terms of individual human beings.

Futurists are fairly accurate in pointing out trends that are making society more competitive, but they seem to have missed a "big picture" development. There is certainly a lot of good in some of the trends transforming the world, but many of them are creating a world where it's easier for cunning to beat ability; i.e., for Cain to kill Abel.

Even the very concept of a megatrend plays to Cain's strengths. Unscramble the word "mega" and you get "game." To Cain, keeping up with every trend is a kind of game. Whether it's good or evil, wise or foolish, permanent or faddish, Cain will go with the flow, ride the wave, stay at the cutting edge. Pick your cliché. In contrast, Abel is more concerned with being right than being "with it," which is why he is often viewed as "out of it" in today's culture.

Here are ten megatrends that increasingly make the "real world" Cain's world.

1. LITIGATION LARCENY

Our legal system is predicated on the idea that truth, justice, and resolution are at the end of the road when someone sues. Increasingly, though, dishonest Cains travel that road while honest Abels will avoid the trip at all costs. It's meant to be a toll road, but Cain can usually find a lawyer who will take the case on a contingency basis. It's often a case of a Cain hiring another Cain.

"No poet ever interpreted nature as freely as a lawyer interprets truth," observed Jean Giraudoux, the French diplomat and writer. The sad reality is that the United States has more than half the world's lawyer population. A great many of them have only a nominal practice, plenty of time on their hands, and will eagerly file a frivolous lawsuit in hopes that the nuisance value will force a settlement. It's greenmail. People are afraid of being sued, and fearful of the publicity arising from a suit. Abel wants to lead a productive life and values his privacy. By contrast, Cain often enjoys notoriety; he wants people to talk about him. And he will use a lawsuit as a weapon to legally intimidate, threaten, and disrupt a rival. Understandably, the emotional turmoil of litigation is so repugnant to Abel that he'll often pay to get rid of it, justice or no.

2. SENSITIVITY SHARING

Cain loves to learn someone's guilty secrets so he can later use the information as leverage with, or as gossip against, that person. The modern trend toward self-confession makes it much easier for Cain to do his "opposition research."

Kurt Vonnegut observed, "We are what we pretend to be." But it seems that in today's culture, we are what we confess to be. Everyone is encouraged by TV psychobabblers to spill their guts as the first step in healing themselves. If you aren't prepared to face your fears by dwelling on them, if you aren't willing to love yourself candidly and publicly, if you aren't willing to trust strangers with your innermost dreams and fantasies, then you are not going to be invited on TV anytime soon.

Now, this is not to disparage the good work that professional psychiatrists and psychologists do. They truly help countless people. But some TV and radio shrinks who psychoanalyze the whole of society and give out generic advice to "the macho type" or "the woman in your life" or "your inner child" have helped create a never-never land where people who do not know themselves are sharing their anguish with people they barely know and/or shouldn't trust.

This urge to public self-confession has infected business, politics, and our entire society.

It's true that keeping everything inside you, repressing all fears and anxieties, may be harmful. But when bosses encourage employees to "open up" in "quality circles" or in "rap sessions," or when they ask very personal, pointed questions in "informal chats" or "off-the-record interviews," the information that's divulged, often very private and assumed to be confidential, can be devastating to those employees, even if it never leaks out, because they live in fear that the person to whom they confided might break their trust.

Cain will betray that trust without a qualm. In the old days, "sharing" with strangers was not considered a moral imperative. The "strong, silent type" was considered strong partly because he was silent. But this is the Age of Cain, and he wants to share your pain . . . with you and with anyone else if it serves his purpose.

3. POLITICIZATION OF EVERYTHING

In any organization where politics becomes more important than productivity, and where power becomes more the goal than individual excellence, Cain usually rules. He may not know "how to succeed in business without really trying," but he knows how to succeed at playing politics inside a business.

Ideologues have long argued that "everything is political." Whether it's economics, psychology, religion, education, fashion, music, or whatever, they treat every difference of opinion as a contentious referendum on society.

Given that we two authors have worked as political consultants, it may seem odd for us to say this, but, the increasing politicization of society is unhealthy. Not all institutions are meant to be absolute models of participatory democracy. The free market itself is not truly democratic, let alone the banks, businesses, and households that comprise it. So, it doesn't denigrate the value of politics to suggest that politicizing everything makes the "real world" not only competitive, but carnivorously competitive—not just dog eat dog, but dog pack eat dog pack.

4. TELEVISIONIZATION

The ever-growing power of television as a medium, separate from the question of its content, is itself a trend. Because television has become so all-pervasive and powerful, the rest of society has been forced to adjust to it. Corporate executives seem to worry about their image as much as product quality. Politicians speak in seven-second sound bites in hopes of "making the cut" for the evening news. This condensation and simplification of thought is bound to lap over into everyday life; it makes complicated and intelligent ideas "boring" and relatively less important, elevates clichés, and favors those who, like Cain, elevate image over substance.

All in all, it's the "Wonderful World of Cain" when so many can be so manipulated by so few.

Ironically, although the televisionization of culture and politics may be the most influential change in history, the question of how TV has affected us receives little attention on television.

In the late 1940s, few households owned a television set. By the 1950s, the TV set was on in the average U.S. household about four hours a day. Now it's on over seven hours a day. Before television, children learned about the world and about values almost entirely from their own family, their close relatives, schools, religious institutions, and their neighborhoods. Today, through television, children are shaped by influences far outside their immediate environment. And today, of course, there are many more channels than before, and the programming is high impact—fast paced, market tested, and ratings driven.

The rapid pace of television editing—where you see a new image every two seconds—has been one of the most important causes of the shortened attention span of people, especially young people. And a shortened attention span leads to an anxious unwillingness and even an inability to defer gratification. This particularly applies to Cain who wants what he wants, and wants it now.

5. MEDIA MUDSLINGING

The spread of "gotcha journalism" makes it easier for Cain to under-mine rivals by planting stories that might be little more than innuendo, ridicule, or rumor. Many use the pejorative "tabloid journalism" to describe gossipy, scandal-mongering "news," but these print and TV tabloids increasingly drive legitimate news reporting. The tabloids break a story, and the TV network news programs and major newspa-pers pick it up and keep it going.

The old standards of who-what-when-where-why factual reporting are replaced by a ratings-driven gamesmanship of gotcha and "so sue me." One might call it "germalism."

While nearly everyone heralds the proliferation of new media as creating more avenues for the truth to emerge, it's become obvious that it's also easier for half-truths to arise and spread virtually unchal-lenged. Lies jump instantly from one medium to the next, on the Internet, over wires and through cables, without the victim of the lie being able to correct the lie before the damage is done. The medium that was the original source of the lie might take days to issue a cor-rection, retraction, or "clarification" while the original lie is beamed by satellite all over the world. Corrections are made grudgingly, if at all, and when made are often buried obscurely on an inside page or an off-hour on the tube (while the lie itself may have received front-page or prime-time treatment).

This lowering of standards likely has a "halo effect" in the work-place, where lies and rumor become more easily accepted. If the jour-nalistic icons who bring us the "facts" stoop to spreading vague and unsubstantiated "information" as "news coverage," what does that teach Cain? It teaches him that if you do it "right," you can get away with it and even be respected for doing it.

6. BUREAUCRATIZATION

The American philosopher George Santayana died in 1952, but his observation about the nature of bureaucracy needs no updating: "The working of great institutions is mainly the result of a vast mass of routine, petty malice, self-interest, carelessness and sheer mistake. Only a residual fraction is thought."

No wonder Cain is so at home in a bureaucratic maze. The opportunities for self-advancement, for using gossip, flattery, connections, fraud, deceit, blame, public relations and private relations are truly endless. The more bureaucratic an organization is, the less "ability" (in the nonbureaucratic sense of the word) stands any chance of prevailing.

Abel's more open nature and his drive to do the right or innovative thing is out of place in a bureaucracy; it threatens the status quo, which, as someone once observed, lives on long after the quo has lost its status.

Cain knows that those who thrive in an advanced bureaucracy are those who never take chances and who do the safe, conventional thing. If you make an unorthodox decision and something goes wrong, you are stuck out on a limb with no defense. But if you make an ordinary, routine decision—the kind of decision that every other bureaucrat makes—and something goes wrong, you can always defend your actions by pointing out that you simply made the most "sensible" (i.e., least risky) choice available. What bureaucrat is going to criticize this standard of decision making? As former president Bush was fond of saying, "It wouldn't be prudent."

Despite all the futurist talk about how decentralization is the prevailing trend of our time, the tendency of any bureaucracy is to grow and grow and grow, like cancer. We are still living in the most bureaucratic age in human history, and Cain thrives in that jungle.

7. POLLING AND OTHER PSEUDOSCIENCE

To the extent that polling can be used to manipulate and mislead, rather than reflect legitimate public opinion, it is a powerful new weapon in Cain's arsenal.

"A lot of serious mistakes are made by viewing polling as an all-knowing Ouija board that can foretell the future," explains political consultant Joseph Gaylord. "Sometimes pollsters seem to use their numbers as wizards must have used their crystal balls: to assert their authority over mere mortals who have nothing to offer but common sense."

Indeed, a pollster can aptly be described as a "wizard of odds." In both politics and business, pollsters try to act as the unofficial spokesman for "the voters" or "today's consumers," and try to set strategy for all-important marketing decisions. But the idea that polling is a reliable forecaster of future elections and consumer behavior has quite often proved to be disastrously wrong. The fiasco in launching New Coke, despite millions spent on market research beforehand, is a classic example.

Poll results can be misleading for many reasons: the sample of people surveyed might not be representative, the questions might be phrased poorly, people lie to the pollster, people lie to themselves, etc. Regardless of accuracy, Cain loves polls because he sees them as a way he can

- manipulate public opinion
- excuse himself if a strategy turns out to be wrong
- impress people by having "inside information."

There are other kinds of pseudoscience used in marketing—mostly perversions of sociology and psychology—and the following graph proves how this phenomenon is working to Cain's advantage.

TRENDS PROVING THAT CUNNING HAS OVERTAKEN ABILITY

Index of Composite Indicators 1958-2000

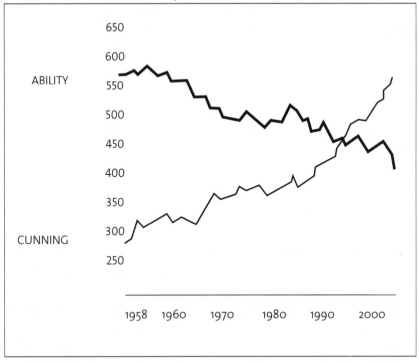

A widening gap is revealed by comparing two "success" factors studied by the Parasocial Unit of Ergo Econometric Systems, Inc.

NOTE: Ability was measured by employee aptitude tests cross-referenced with data supplied by confidential personnel evaluations. Cunning was calculated as the composite index of nonproductivity promotions and unpunished misconduct as reported by educational, corporate, and political entities and related to nonmerit advancement and relative income growth.

As you can quickly see by a glance at the graph, since 1960 cunning as a predictor of success has increased by a factor of two, while ability has declined by more than a third.

This clearly proves our thesis, except for one problem—it's complete nonsense. We made it up.

Read it again. How could intangibles like cunning and ability ever be scientifically measured? This isn't methodology . . . it's *mythodology*. Yet, for a moment, it looked kind of convincing.

This is the kind of pseudoscientific persuasion that Cain will use to bolster an argument. Sometimes Cain might not even know that his "data" or "proof" is nonsense, and he doesn't really care. He only cares whether it suits his purpose. Remember, from Cain's point of view, con artistry is also a science.

8. CULTURE ROT

Mass culture has undergone a dramatic transition, a sea change that favors Cain. Popular culture now routinely mocks and undermines basic values: the work ethic, faith, family, honesty, integrity. It bombards us with carnality and blurs the distinction between right and wrong. Judgment, in the sense of making distinctions between good and bad, is no longer treated as a mark of good character. Instead, it is condemned as "judgmental." How dare you judge another person who may only be doing his own thing? What makes your thing superior to, or better than, someone else's thing? A strong indication of popular culture's ascendant power and influence is the fact that most people are defensive, if not discombobulated, when assaulted by this kind of reasoning.

While it's true that a principal aim of art is to challenge conventional mores—to provoke people to think—we shouldn't kid ourselves about the profound metamorphosis that's taken place in mass culture. The old black-and-white programming (in terms of both film and ethics) has become today's programming of blood-red gore and all-gray ethics.

Pauline Kael noted this in her book, *I Lost It at the Movies*, "What this generation was bred to at television's knee was not wisdom but cynicism."

Just as military technology has outpaced the morality of those who make war, so too has the technology and sophistication of mass culture outpaced the ethical sense of those who make money by marketing "art" to the lowest common denominator.

Obviously, this trend is to Cain's advantage. He's not restrained by

Abel's sense of decency. For Cain, ratings or survey data provide all the justification he needs for a decision.

As mass culture makes people more susceptible to manipulation and base appeals, Cain's amoral crassness becomes less and less offensive to his colleagues. In fact, it begins to seem just plain sensible.

"Years ago, critic Lionel Trilling wondered what would happen if the adversary culture of artistic elites pervaded all of society. Well, it would look pretty much like what we have now," observed columnist John Leo, "a culture that celebrates impulse over restraint, notoriety over achievement, rule breaking over rule keeping and incendiary expression over minimal civility."

9. MASS MOVEMENT

In our mobile, transient society more and more people move to wherever new, high-paying job opportunities beckon. But within this seemingly positive trend, there is opportunity for Cain to do mischief. As it becomes more acceptable for people to relocate and seek new employment, Cain is less fearful about being exposed and forced out of his current job. He knows he can always move elsewhere, leave his reputation behind without arousing suspicion, and then reinvent himself. Even though we live in the age of the computer and the Internet, both of which make it easier than ever to check on a person's background, few companies bother to do so. They may be afraid of being sued for invading someone's privacy, or they may simply feel that it isn't proper to pry into someone's personal life. In any case, there is a decline in accountability when more and more people can escape the consequences of their actions by disappearing into a black hole of anonymity.

10. COMPETITIVENESS AS THE NEW MORALITY

We live in a competitive society, and competition can be healthy for both individuals and society . . . if it takes place in an arena where rules and self-restraint limit its most extreme practices. Unfortunately, healthy competition has too often become destructive competitiveness in modern society. It is one thing for a young girl to compete aggressively for a place on the cheerleading squad; it is something quite different when the girl's mother tries to hire a hitman to kill a potential rival. An extreme and unrepresentative case? Of course, it is. But in somewhat moderated forms, this "success at all costs" mentality has become widespread. Cheating and intimidation are common in sports, government, politics, business, and nearly every walk of life.

Cain thrives in this kind of vicious atmosphere. If the only thing that really matters is competitiveness, if that is the dominant ethic (or lack thereof), Cain can use his favorite tools—paranoia, fear, envy, greed—to pit people against one another. To repeat, this is not an indictment of healthy competition. But reality is reality; in any good trend, there is also some bad. And Cain is sure to find it and exploit it.

✦ ✦ ✦

CHAPTER 16

Advice for Abel:
27 Keys to Combating Cain

In his book, *Introducing the Brain,* John Pfeiffer observed, "Give a chimpanzee a few bananas, a peaceful stretch of jungle and plenty of bananas, and it will live happily for the rest of its life. Give a man an environment correspondingly idyllic, say a Garden of Eden, and he will get into trouble. Getting into trouble is our genius and glory as a species."

"Getting into trouble" may be the perfect phrase for summing up much of human history, but *causing* trouble, and *enjoying* the misery of others in trouble, is not the same thing. That's Cain's nature; it's not the essence of human nature.

We know that Cain is a person whose behavior is based on calculating and ruthless self-interest. His narrow focus on what benefits him, even at the expense of others, makes him a particularly dangerous adversary. As we have pointed out, Cain will lie, cheat, steal credit, unfairly blame others, and generally manipulate those around him in order to succeed, and he will do this without remorse or any real sense of guilt because he has a great capacity to rationalize his actions. Abel is someone who has been conditioned, by his own nature and experience, to assume that good behavior will automatically be rewarded and bad behavior will be punished. Abel believes in behaving "decently."

He is considerate of others. And his accepting and unsuspicious nature can be easily exploited by Cain.

Assuming that you, the reader, are a well-meaning Abel, undoubtedly you'd like to better understand how to prevent a Cain from causing trouble for you. To that end, we've devised a checklist of practical steps you can take to help figure out your options and the best course of action.

Before going into combat with a Cain, ponder the following.

1. BE HONEST ABOUT YOUR OWN MOTIVES

"Nothing is so easy as to deceive one's self," wrote Demosthenes, the great Athenian orator, "for what we wish, we readily believe." Just because you're not a despicable Cain, someone utterly selfish and mean, doesn't mean that you are pure in your intentions and automatically right in any dispute with a Cain.

We suggest being *painfully* honest in examining your own motives because it is often a painful procedure. No one likes to discover that he or she is criticizing someone out of jealousy, or to hide one's own shortcomings, or to rationalize one's own greed or lust for power. But that may be the case. It's so much easier to depict a rival as unethical, disloyal, and undeserving than to admit that one's own view is colored by self-interest.

An amusing example of this kind of rationalization was in *Roughing It* by Mark Twain: "At noon I observed a bevy of nude native young ladies bathing in the sea, and went and sat down on their clothes to keep them from being stolen."

Before harshly judging someone else's motives, look in the mirror and ask yourself some penetrating questions: What are your true motives? Do you despise someone because they're thwarting your ambitions? Are you envious of the advantages a rival enjoys? H. G. Wells warned, "Moral indignation is jealousy with a halo." Are you yourself beyond reproach, or are you doing the very things that you accuse Cain of doing? Think long and hard.

2. AVOID DEMONIZATION

Do not get corrupted by hatred. Just because someone is a rotten character doesn't mean that you should ascribe satanic qualities to him. First of all, you should not assume someone is a Cain unless you are certain. "Beyond a shadow of a doubt" would be a good standard. It's far too easy to conclude that a colleague is an ambitious competitor and thus a rival and thus an adversary and thus an enemy and thus an untrustworthy person who should be viewed with contempt. This kind of escalating, emotional reasoning is fueled by fear and perhaps envy and is ultimately self-destructive.

It is particularly dangerous to voice your opinion about someone being a Cain if you only have circumstantial evidence. Do not make accusations that could come back to haunt you. For example, we've used the word "evil" a few times in this book in referring to the nature of a Cain, but keep in mind that we are describing a nameless, hypothetical person. You should not bandy such words about in conversation or resort to name-calling. It's important to keep the Cain problem in perspective; you're not trying to start a witch hunt, you're just trying to cope with an unprincipled person.

3. DON'T OBSESS

Assuming that you've accurately identified a true Cain, and assuming that you are motivated by good intentions, now what? First, you should realize that one potential pitfall is becoming obsessed with Cain to the point where you overreact to his every move and neglect your duties. Just as villains are often the most mesmerizing characters in movies, so, too, can a Cain draw much of your conscious attention. If you spend too much time worrying about what Cain is up to, or what Cain said or did, you can lose perspective and get so stressed out that you alienate your colleagues. Stay focused on the important things in your life: work, family, friends, learning, community. . . . Don't let your rivalry with a Cain turn into a consuming passion.

How do you determine whether you're spending a sensible amount of time worrying about Cain or whether you're becoming obsessed with him? Chances are, you'll have a friend, colleague, or family member in whom you will have confided your worries about Cain. If you trust their counsel, ask them if they think you've become too focused on Cain. Since you are the one raising the issue, they should feel a little more comfortable in giving you a candid answer. However, if you don't agree with their guidance, or if you don't have such a confidant, you need to ask yourself some questions: How much time do you spend worrying about Cain? How often does your concentration wander toward Cain? Are you losing sleep over Cain? How much of your conversation is about Cain? Once you complete this mental inventory, you might come to realize that at least part of your problem is of your own making. If you have allowed him to become an obsession, then your hypersensitivity and overreaction have made you more vulnerable to him. Don't let your obsession become the issue with others.

4. DON'T BECOME "THE PROBLEM"

There is a great danger that if you overreact you may be perceived by others as a chronic complainer. Cain is very adept at deceiving others and can easily use your grumbling to characterize you as a "whiner." If your constant criticism, not Cain's behavior, becomes the issue, then you run the risk of being marked as a "problem" rather than a "problem solver." This is another illustration of Abel's Axiom: Being Right Can Be Wrong. It is a simple truth, but one that many people overlook, that those you work with, or for, react positively to others who make their life easier, not harder. Very few people welcome more problems being dumped in their laps. Think back to Case Study 13 in which Vernon tried to steal credit for work done by Lisa and Leslie. Lisa and Leslie's hasty and ill-considered response—shrill, petty in tone, and accusatory without real proof—created a headache for their manager, hardly the kind of behavior likely to make their boss think better of them.

If you become the constant bearer of unpleasant news, especially if the news is repetitive (i.e., "Cain is a rat!"), your boss or coworkers are likely to tune you out and, eventually, start avoiding you altogether. The fundamental philosophical principle of the Greeks was "Nothing to excess." Always keep it in mind, no matter how frustrated you become with Cain. If you let your carping become the issue, Cain wins.

5. DON'T SINK TO CAIN'S LEVEL

No matter how vile Cain's conduct may be, no matter how much he poses a threat to good people, do not adopt the end-justifies-the-means rationale for acting like him to counteract him. For example, don't use entrapment, don't use surveillance. If you resort to unethical behavior in order to defeat Cain, it's really a victory for his worldview, namely, that it's a dog-eat-dog world and winning is all that matters. Hold on to your decency and stay true to your sense of honor. Cains come and go, but you continue to live with yourself.

And there is a very practical reason to forgo unscrupulous tactics: They often backfire. The ironic truth is, they *frequently* backfire when employed by honorable people, because they don't have the ruthless mind-set often required to successfully implement manipulative schemes. Abels usually can't imagine and anticipate possible snags in an unfair tactic, how to squirm out of blame, how to minimize the damage done if caught, how to brazenly change the issue to spread blame around, and all the other Cain-like dodges we have covered in this book. For many reasons, it's best to be resolute in trying to win fairly. Over the long run, it's probably the most effective tactic, and it's best for your self-esteem anyway. As baseball great Jackie Robinson said in his book, *I Never Had It Made*, "The most luxurious possession, the richest treasure anybody has, is his personal dignity."

6. NEVER UNDERESTIMATE A CAIN

Just as you shouldn't overestimate Cain to the point of becoming obsessed and overly fearful of what he might do, it's equally true that you shouldn't underestimate him, either. Oscar Wilde once joked, "I can resist everything except temptation." That's a pretty fair way to describe Cain's outlook. He is inexorably drawn to the temptations of power, money, fame, and vices generally. And he is quite willing to work overtime in plotting and scheming to pursue these interests. Indeed, he might be willing to play any dirty trick—including stabbing an Abel in the back—to get his way.

Never imagine that you're competing with Cain on an even playing field. He's going to do his darnedest to make sure everything favors him: the terrain, the spectators, the weapons, and the timing of the match. The one thing you can count on, since he is constantly scheming, is that he will likely have the advantage of surprise. He is not going to volunteer for a duel; he wants an ambush. So, be realistic. Never underestimate what a devious, single-minded person can do.

7. DON'T CORNER A CAIN

As we mentioned earlier, don't make the mistake of cornering a Cain unless you're prepared to become a target for future revenge. Just as cornering a rat will make it turn and attack you, so will Cain attack—although not necessarily right away—if you openly confront and embarrass him. This is true even if you privately, discreetly let him know that you see through him and that you know he's done unethical things of which you sincerely disapprove. You might as well paint a bull's-eye on your forehead and wait for him to get even with you.

Cain will be intensely threatened even if you broach the question of his behavior with humor—because now you *know* about him, and your awareness is an ever-present threat to his ambitions. He cannot tolerate the idea that someone is implicitly threatening to expose him. Cain finds that particularly frightening because he knows that if he had a similar opportunity to hurt a rival, he'd do so without hesitation.

Even if you never tell or threaten to tell anyone about his true nature, he will still consider your knowledge a personal threat. Steve Martin, the comedian/actor/director, once said: "There is one thing I would break up over, and that is if [my girlfriend] caught me with another woman. I won't stand for that."

In a noncomical confrontation, Cain is likely to lash out at his accuser with a nastiness that is intended to convince Abel to never try cornering him again. This is not to say that you should let Cain get away with unethical conduct, but rather that you should not challenge Cain unless you are prepared for the aftermath. An old adage warns: "Never strike at a king unless you are certain to kill him."

The point is, cornering Cain should be attempted only if you've thought it through and you're confident of prevailing in the long run. Don't rashly decide to confront him simply because in your frustration you can't stand seeing him get away with his chicanery a moment longer.

8. SET YOUR GOAL—CAREFULLY

You can't expect to develop a winning strategy to thwart Cain if you're not clear about what constitutes winning. Do you hope to get him fired, demoted, transferred, investigated, arrested? Think carefully about what is appropriate and realistic. Try to discern the difference between your emotional longing for what seems like justice, which might involve punishing Cain for past misdeeds, and more practical considerations; for example, keeping damage to yourself and others to a minimum.

Be sure to take into account what might happen if you achieve your goal. If you succeed in getting Cain fired, anticipate what he might try to do to exact revenge. If you get him transferred, does he then try to use the powers of his new department to get even with you? If you succeed in having him investigated, what accusations might he contrive to deny culpability? If you expose him, how far are you willing to go to substantiate your claims?

These potential dangers can be most easily seen in high profile political conflicts. During the Watergate scandals of the Nixon administration, when Martha Mitchell, wife of Attorney General John Mitchell, began talking to the press about some of the questionable and illegal activities taking place, she was viciously attacked by the administration as an alcoholic and "emotionally disturbed" woman. And when John Dean became the star witness before the Senate investigating committee, he faced the same kind of attack—he was attacked as a "liar" who was trying to protect himself because, they alleged, he himself had been involved in and had even directed the illegal activities. The same tactics of investigate, attack, and impugn the motives or behavior of your accusers—your "enemies"—have been employed relentlessly by some Clinton political operatives. For example, Monica Lewinsky was a "liar" who was "stalking" the President. Your life may not be lived on the same grand public scale as Martha Mitchell, John Dean, or Monica Lewinsky (at least, we hope not), but in your own world, you can be vulnerable to the same sort of revenge and counterattacks if you take on a Cain.

Try to think through all the ramifications before settling on your ultimate goal. Consider not just what you are prepared to do to win, but equally what you're prepared to lose if the fight gets ugly. Make sure you are willing to pay the price of victory in what might become a mud-wrestling contest with no referee.

9. DON'T EXPECT A RATIONAL OPPONENT

Cain's brain is wired very differently from ordinary people, as evidenced by the fact that he actually enjoys lying, cheating, and abusing others. He's sadistic to the point of risking his own well-being if the risk enables him to lord it over other people. And he is oblivious to his own duplicity. As the great psychologist and psychiatrist, Carl Jung, explained, "People will do anything, no matter how absurd, in order to avoid facing their own soul."

What all this means is that you can't easily outmaneuver him by relying on accepted rules, or appease him with incentives, or isolate him with explicit warnings. Even though it might obviously be in his best interest to obey the rules, to be guided by new incentives, or to steer clear of past mistakes, remember that he is ruled by reckless internal urges. His "logic" is irrational. Don't expect it to be otherwise.

10. DON'T TRUST AN ALLIANCE WITH CAIN

Stalin signed a peace pact with Hitler, only to be surprised by the invasion of the Soviet Union not long afterward. Both were ultra Cains, of course, but the same threat presents itself when a fearful Abel tries to prosper by hooking up with a Cain. If Abel subordinates himself to Cain he may ascend the organizational ladder with him, but at what cost? He loses his self-respect by tolerating the abuse he receives from Cain, and by being a party to the abuse of others. He worries about being exposed for complicity in unethical behavior, the least of which would be rumormongering, ridicule of decent people, shirking responsibility, and deceiving others. And, if suddenly Cain needs a scapegoat, someone to blame for mistakes, negligence, or shoddy work, Abel may be the fall guy. Martha Mitchell, the outspoken wife of Nixon's Attorney General during the Watergate scandal, described the president in precisely those terms: Nixon "bleeds people," she told reporter Helen Thomas. "He draws every drop of blood and then drops them from a cliff. He'll blame any person he can put his foot on."

The point is, Cain can't be trusted. He won't be loyal if it's inconvenient to be so. And jettisoning an aide or ally is not only easy for him to do, it's something he might take pride in doing because it shows what a tough competitor he is, what a ruthless, realistic "manager" he can be in difficult situations.

11. DON'T SUCCUMB TO TEMPTATION

As we've pointed out, one of Cain's common tactics is to co-opt opponents by appealing to their greed and buying them off. He might even entice you with a hypothetical offer that he has no intention or ability of actually fulfilling. "We should help each other," he might say in a conspiratorial tone. "Would you like a free vacation to Europe—on the company's nickel? Let me see what I can do. But don't mention this to anyone. You watch my back, and I'll watch yours."

Once you say yes to him, you're on the slipperiest of slopes. You have been compromised, and Cain has you trapped in a downward spiral. You've agreed to a secret arrangement with an unspoken promise: "We're partners in a scheme." In reality, he wants to know your price. How much is your independence and integrity worth to you?

When he succeeds in buying someone off, it confirms in his own mind that everyone is just as amoral as he is. Cain especially relishes buying someone off *cheaply* because that degrades the other person all the more and makes Cain himself feel morally superior.

If Cain unexpectedly offers you some choice seats at a sporting event, some Cuban cigars, or he picks up your tab at dinner, be warned: You're being set up for the time when he will ask a favor that you would ordinarily reject. Will you feel free to spurn his request if you accept his gifts? Consider what Aristotle said: "I count him braver who overcomes his desires than him who conquers his enemies; for the hardest victory is the victory over self." Don't allow yourself to be compromised by a Cain. Never accept gifts when you distrust the motives of the giver.

12. DON'T FALL FOR FLATTERY

People often see flattery directed at others as transparently insincere, while flattery of one's self is perceived as well-meaning, perhaps even overdue, praise.

Earlier we pointed out that when people flatter others, even tongue in cheek, they're often called charming. True charm, of course, emanates from sincerity, not calculation. Resist the tendency to trust a Cain who flatters you because the truth is, he's flattering you for an obvious reason: He wants something from you, perhaps not immediately, but be assured that at some point he will ask you for something that will serve his self-interest. The favor might come at the expense of others, or yourself. Be on guard. When you're flattered by Cain, don't waste time weighing the correctness of his praise; instead, question what angle he might be playing in hopes of gaining something. Keep in mind, too, that it is hardly flattering to be thought of as someone who is susceptible to flattery.

13. UNDERSTAND THE POWER MOTIVE

Lord Acton, the English historian most noted for his warning that "power tends to corrupt and absolute power corrupts absolutely," put that truism in perspective when he wrote: "History is not a web woven with innocent hands. Among all the causes which degrade and demoralize men, power is the most constant and the most active." As we've observed, Cain craves power, and will readily use it to inflict pain on those who obstruct his ambition.

Abel will also seek power at times, and to some extent is likely to be a little corrupted by it. If nothing else, power gratifies the ego. But when Abel seeks power, he usually has mixed motives, some of them good. An Abel might sincerely want to accomplish something in particular that would at the same time benefit the greater good. Cain wants power for its own sake. For him, it's not a means to an altruistic end; it is the end itself. He wants power over others because it feeds his hunger for self-importance and also permits him to control others for his own benefit.

It's important to understand this in coping with a Cain. Don't make the mistake of believing that Cain will mellow or be appeased if granted more power. His power lust will never be satisfied. Cain is an aggressor, and like any aggressor, he always wants the land bordering his.

14. DON'T BE FOOLED BY CAIN'S CONTRITION

If Cain has been caught in a scam that he can't plausibly talk his way out of, he might, as a last resort, apologize and promise to turn over a new leaf. Out of compassion, many an Abel will fall for this and hope for redemption. But while a Cain will *occasionally* change, perhaps in a spiritual conversion or some traumatic revelation, chances are it's an act. A chameleon can change colors but it can't change into a Saint Bernard.

This advice may sound cynical and unfeeling; nonetheless, it's true that it's best not to rely on Cain actually changing in any *meaningful* way. He may be entirely sincere in promising that what he did will never happen again, but what he probably means is that he'll never be *caught* doing it again. That is not genuine repentance.

Even though you might feel sympathy for Cain if he's asking for mercy—and while it's fine to understand that Cain might actually be suffering at some level because deep down he realizes that he's a deplorable character incapable of true decency—don't expect Cain to convert and suddenly become trustworthy. If you do, you're just making yourself vulnerable to his future gambits.

15. DON'T PROVIDE GRIST FOR THE MILL

Once it's known that a shifty, conniving person is at large within an organization, it's natural that he becomes the focus of conversation. Some of the talk is nasty gossip; much is idle speculation. People will be careful not to disparage Cain to his allies, of course, but generally, people who've been insulted or threatened by him will find others who have suffered or observed similar abuse, and they'll vent their resentment, confident that the gossip will not get back to Cain.

Some of this chatter about Cain can't be dismissed as mere gossip, because in many instances it's the sharing of information for mutual protection or to minimize the damage that Cain is doing to morale. But be careful about believing, let alone passing on, disparaging stories. Since Cain is in fact guilty of so many offenses, it's easy to believe anything that belittles him, but this doesn't mean that everything said about him is true. Try not to depend solely on the word of others. Remember, the other person may be another Cain who is trying to manipulate and mislead you for reasons of his own.

Often the "bad boy" image of Cain is projected by him to intimidate others. He might feel that having a reputation for unscrupulousness and aggressiveness will make others wary of crossing him. Abel can't even comprehend this kind of mentality; he suffers when others think him unkind and egotistical. Cain is very different. He will even boast of his infamy to associates and subordinates. He'll exaggerate or weave out of whole cloth some story where he acted with absolute disregard for what other people think. We know of one high-ranking executive who always claimed credit for laying off or forcing out an employee, even though in nearly every case he had absolutely nothing to do with it. In his mind, he wanted others to perceive him as having the power of life and death, so to speak, over their careers.

To repeat, don't assume that everything unfavorable said about Cain is true. You do not want to make the mistake of slandering someone or be caught passing on gossip that turns out to be false. You also don't want to make Cain larger than life. You and your associates should not get so worked up over his imagined misdeeds that you are too intimidated to deal with him or too distracted to anticipate the new schemes he may be plotting.

16. BEWARE OF CAIN MINDING YOUR BUSINESS

Most Abels are raised with the admonition, "Mind your own business." This blunt advice sums up a lot of parental wisdom: Don't stick your nose where it doesn't belong; respect the privacy of others; concentrate on improving your own work; and, of course, always remember that curiosity killed the cat.

Cain thinks your parents are naive. He believes that minding your business is a part of *his* business. And if Cain is caught intruding in someone else's business, he will be armed with any number of rationalizations: He is just doing research, monitoring quality control, or keeping an eye on the competition.

Ordinarily, Cain will investigate rivals in ways that can't be held against him in any formal inquiry. He'll cultivate sources close to those in power who will gossip with him, keep him posted on new developments, and perhaps even show him sensitive or confidential documents. If expedient, however, he may resort to hiring professional investigators to do "discreet research" or, perhaps on his own, resort to illegal surveillance.

If Cain is asking odd or suspicious questions, or trying to acquire sensitive documents or inside information, it could portend his trying to use that inside knowledge to manipulate or coerce people for his own devious purposes. It might be something as ordinary as Cain's sudden interest in someone else's expense report, which could tell him if someone has been overcharging the company or, more dangerous yet, something about a fellow employee's habits or personal life.

CASE STUDY 29

Tony and Kevin were the top two candidates for a promotion, which meant a better title, a better salary, better perks, better everything, and Tony was determined to come out the winner.

Over the past year, Tony had noticed that Kevin was away from work for several hours every two weeks. When he asked Kevin's administrative assistant what was going on, she casually said, "Oh, he's had quite a few doctor's appointments."

"That's too bad," Tony said, and then asked in an innocent voice, "Who's his doctor?" The administrative assistant made the mistake of telling him the name.

Tony went back to his office and checked out the doctor's name on the Internet, discovering that the doctor was a psychiatrist who specialized in treating substance abuse problems.

That's all Tony needed to know. He casually mentioned the fact to a few people, and the information spread through the company like wildfire. Some said Kevin had "a drinking problem"; others said he was "hooked on drugs."

Whatever the truth, the story planted just enough doubt in the minds of higher-ups to tip the balance in Tony's favor.

Given all this, how worried should you be about Cain? Are you his target? Is he busy creating a dossier on you? You can drive yourself crazy if you start worrying about every conversation Cain might be having with someone in a position of influence or with access to inside information. Paranoia is self-defeating. This is not to say that ignorance is bliss. Ignoring clear signs that Cain is poking into things outside of his defined responsibilities could prove dangerous for you and for others in your organization. If you can figure out in advance what Cain is trying to do, you'll be better able to detect, prevent, counteract, or at least minimize his stratagem. Mind your own business, but don't ignore Cain's attempts to mind someone else's business, especially yours.

17. DON'T GET SUCKED IN TO MIND GAMES

If an Abel admonishes Cain to "Mind your own business," Cain's unspoken thought is, "But, manipulating your mind *is* my business."

Cain delights in playing mind games with Abel for two reasons.

1. He feels intellectually superior to Abel since Abel is less adept at the kind of "gotcha" banter that Cain enjoys and employs (much as a carnival barker uses insults and other personal remarks to lure people into rigged games of chance).
2. He is better able to appraise Abel as a competitor—to find his weak points, and perhaps even an "Achilles' heel"—by gauging Abel's reaction to provocative comments.

For example, Cain might let loose a torrent of insults at Abel in an attempt to create "cognitive dissonance," mental confusion, which could help Cain evaluate several things: Abel's ability to cope with pressure and criticism, his level of confidence, his values, and his willingness to fight back. Immediately after subjecting Abel to this compulsory psychoanalysis, Cain might even apologize to Abel. "Sorry, I was bothered by something else."

Abel, relieved that Cain is less vicious and irrational than first feared, might well sympathize with Cain and assure him that the episode is forgiven and will be forgotten. But Cain certainly won't forget what he learned in the mind game, nor will he be afraid to try yet another mind game on that same forgiving Abel if it suits his purposes or his mood. After all, Cain gets the same kind of rush from toying with an unsuspecting Abel that a chessmaster feels when declaring, "Checkmate!" It's a mastery of mind over mind. The fact that it's done at the expense of someone else's emotional well-being makes it all the more satisfying because to Cain winning is all about making other people lose. He really believes that "there is no substitute for victory" in any competition—not love, not truth, not the greatest good for the greatest number, nor any other moral or philosophical principle.

When Cain plays mind games, it's not "playing" in the sense of recreation. It's part of his work. It's learning the weaknesses of people, calculating what makes them tick and what conceivably might make them give up their principles and subordinate themselves to him.

A favorite little trick of one Cain is to ask a talented subordinate—a possible upcoming rival—for a favor and, in the middle of the conversation, abruptly ask, "You like your job, don't you?" The threat is obvious, yet if this Cain were challenged, he can easily defend himself as someone who was merely and genuinely concerned about the employee's feelings. Maybe Cain was thinking about offering the person a chance to change jobs for the better. In reality, this particular Cain is usually uninterested in the favor itself; he really wants to determine if the person he's dealing with will cave in to the implied threat. If so, Cain has learned that the person can be manipulated by fear.

If Abel understands this fact about Cain, he might decide to outfox him; for example, answering questions with sly, misleading, or obtuse answers. In the example just cited, the person threatened might be tempted to make his own implied threat: "I love my job. I know you love yours, and the way [your boss] has been talking about you, I hope you get to keep it."

But this accomplishes nothing more than alerting Cain to danger, either from his own boss (if the statement is true) or from the subordinate himself (who is now identified as someone willing to fight back). Cain has been forewarned and forearmed for the battle.

Cain has more patience at playing these games than Abel because, ultimately, he has something to gain from these games. Burrowing into the minds of others, if only to confuse them and keep them guessing about his motives, can work to Cain's benefit. While Abel might think his own "crafty" conversation reveals nothing of importance to Cain, he's wrong. Just by making this effort, he is disclosing something valuable to Cain. Abel is letting Cain know that Cain has "got" to him. Cain now knows Abel wants to compete with him.

For Cain, this is no "game." He's not interested in mock combat. Instead, he wants to mock his enemies, and by mocking them, rebuke them. And to him, his enemies are all who dare challenge him.

Don't play pointless mind games with Cain. It will only make him more determined than ever to hurt you, and hurt you sooner rather than later. Don't take the bait when he flatters, insults, gossips, threatens, or offers any kind of temptation. Don't be afraid, or seem to be afraid, to talk with Cain, but you'll be better off trying to keep conversation with him to a minimum. The more involved you are with Cain, especially if he's trying to trifle with your mind, the more your emotions will warp your perspective and judgment. A past president of the American College of Trial Lawyers, Joseph Ball, once explained, "The more I become involved emotionally in my client's cause, the less I am able to do for him." This is just as true about dealing with a Cain. If you allow yourself to be drawn into mind games that churn your emotions, you will be less able to think in a clear, calm, sensible way about your predicament.

18. THINK BEFORE YOU WRITE

Earlier, we pointed out that Cain avoids putting his thoughts in writing for many reasons, but mainly because it doesn't allow him the wiggle room to pretend that he agrees with everyone on all sides of a dispute. Also, it makes it easy for an opponent to use his words against him later, especially if, like Cain, a critic is willing to distort the intended meaning.

Cain appreciates the wry advice given to politicians for avoiding trouble: Never write when you can speak, never speak when you can nod, never nod when you can wink. As former California Governor Edmund "Pat" Brown noted, "A little vagueness goes a long way in this business."

Abel will seldom triumph over Cain by adopting Cain's cynical tactics, but it pays to *understand* Cain's tactics—in this case, his aversion to committing himself in writing—in order to avoid being duped and manipulated by him.

And it is only sensible to be conscientious about what you write yourself, knowing that Cain might be looking to twist your meaning and use it against you. Before submitting something you've written, something irretrievable, review it first with Cain in mind, perhaps with the help of a trusted associate. Try to read it from Cain's combative point of view. Don't be overly sensitive about what someone might say in criticism, because anything can be nitpicked to death if people are so inclined, but you will be better off anticipating trouble than not. If you're not prepared for Cain, you can be surprised, hurt, and embarrassed by the unexpected.

Also, don't hesitate to create a written record for the purpose of protecting yourself. Documentation can sometimes be a life—and a job—saver.

If you strongly suspect that Cain may be guilty of harassment, theft, fraud, or other unethical or illegal conduct, you should keep notes on the matter and a copy or record of any evidence. At some point in the future, you'll have to decide whether you have sufficient evidence, circumstantial or otherwise, to confide in a superior, a lawyer, or possibly someone in law enforcement. Any reservations about informing the proper authority should not deter you from at least making notes of the relevant facts: dates, people, documents. If necessary, they may help you substantiate the truth. You don't want any dispute to become a matter of Cain's word versus yours, or Cain's word versus some other innocent person.

If you do keep such a record, you should be discreet about it. There is an old rule: No more than two people can be trusted to keep a secret. If I tell you something, and it then leaks out, I know who told. But if I tell two people, I can't know whether you or the other person had the loose lips. One of President Lyndon Johnson's favorite tricks to test whether a potential candidate for a position in his administration had discretion and could be trusted was to tell the candidate a supposed "secret." The secret would be false, and Johnson would never mention it to anyone else. If the information then appeared in the media, Johnson would know who leaked it.

The fact is that most people gossip freely. Even your best friend might well confide whatever you tell him or her to another friend, who then might pass the information along to a third friend, and so on, and so on, and so on, ad infinitum. The knowledge that you are keeping a record of Cain's suspicious behavior could spread to a point where others see you as a Linda Tripp wannabe—the woman who secretly taped Monica Lewinsky in the Clinton sex scandal and for many became a symbol of treachery, a rat who betrayed the trust of a friend.

So, be cautious about what you put in writing, and this includes e-mail. You may think you're merely expressing your thoughts to a trusted friend or associate and assume that your words disappear into the electronic ether. T'ain't necessarily so. Not only might your friend save and share your recorded comments with other interested parties—one of whom, in turn, might share it with Cain or an ally of his—but Cain could also use a techie friend to retrieve past missives that you thought were deleted and examine them as well. It's not difficult for computer detectives to retrieve documents that were supposedly disposed of in the electronic trash.

If you're in a serious fight with Cain, it's best to follow this adage: Don't say or write anything that you wouldn't want to see on the front page of your local newspaper. If you follow this advice, you've acted with reasonable care. Nonetheless, you still have to worry about your words being taken out of context or distorted beyond recognition. Isn't that enough?

19. DON'T FALL FOR EMPTY WORDS

In *The Organization Man*, a classic of business sociology published in 1956, author William H. Whyte, Jr. was prescient in warning that

English was "being slighted" by business and schools alike. "If technicians of 'business writing' and the psychologists have been able to denature English into a 'communication' science, it is because the greater relevance of English has been left undrawn," he wrote. "And this, in the long run, means a less useful English."

The proliferation of jargon and euphemisms in business and most other professions seems to bear him out. As explained earlier, Cain doesn't mind this at all. He wants words to be elastic and slippery, not meaningful, because to him words are weapons for winning, not tools for building—words express intentions, not promises. They reflect what is convenient, not necessarily what is true. Cain values language for getting his way, and since his way is often distinct from the greater good, he values words for manipulating, obfuscating, flattering, appealing to baser emotions, not for persuading with facts and logic nor for appealing to higher aspirations.

Cain doesn't prefer buzzwords just because they seem in vogue; he prefers them because they suit his purposes. Perhaps "cloak and dagger" best describes his attitude about language. He chooses words that *cloak* his true aims or *cloak* reality, or words that serve as a *dagger* against his adversaries. Euphemisms and bureaucratic jargon are cloak words. For example, saying, "He died from friendly fire," instead of, "We accidentally shot one of our own soldiers," cloaks and obscures what really happened. Dagger words are those that stab and gut the competition. Former House Speaker Newt Gingrich once sent a list of adjectives that he urged GOP candidates to use against their opponents, including words like "corrupt" and "radical." In a spirit of nonpartisanship, we should also point out that some Democrats describe every Republican initiative as "reckless" or "extreme."

In the right circumstances, a single word has the power to destroy. In a business conference, Cain might describe one of your proposals as "daring." While that might imply "innovative" or "brave" to some people, it could well suggest "risky" to more conservative business types. If your idea continues to be talked about as "daring" or "risky," it's probably a goner.

Don't allow Cain to define a situation or debate by establishing the ground rules of language. If he calls your idea "daring," challenge him immediately. "It may be new and different, but I'd hardly call it daring." Emphasize the strong points and advantages of your idea, and put the risks in perspective. You might even point out the risks in *not* doing what you propose.

Empty words of promise can be just as effective as derogatory language. A few years ago, a television producer developed a simple technique for recruiting allies at his network. In a conversation with a new employee, he would say, "You know, I've been thinking about putting together a new talk show, and you might have the talent to host it." For months afterward, that simple, vacuous statement (there never was any planned new talk show) guaranteed the producer a strong supporter for whatever he wanted to do.

Always pay close attention to language. Don't let vagueness, empty promises, complexity, clichés, or attack language confuse you, shape your opinions, or manipulate your emotions. Don't let Cain goad you to anger, make you feel insecure, stir empty hopes in you, or control you to any extent by using language in a calculated way.

20. DON'T SWALLOW THE BIG LIE

Size is relative, of course, so what may seem like a whopper of a lie to Abel may seem quite modest to Cain who, after all, considers lying an art form. "The size of the lie is a definite factor in causing it to be believed," Adolf Hitler wrote in *Mein Kampf*, "for the vast masses of a nation are in the depths of their hearts more easily deceived than they are consciously and intentionally bad. The primitive simplicity of their minds renders them a more easy prey to a big lie than a small one, for they themselves often tell little lies but would be ashamed to tell big ones."

Cain may not be as depraved as Hitler, but the argument Hitler made—that most people are more likely to believe a big lie precisely because it's big (i.e., ordinary people can't conceive of anyone making up something so outrageous)—continues to guide many a Cain today. Cain might not consciously think of Hitler's rationale for lying on a grand scale, but over time he notices that naive Abels are much more impressed when a story is embellished and details are exaggerated. Despite the risks in fabricating a story or altering the facts of a narrative, Cain takes a perverse enjoyment in lying. He has so much confidence that others will share his pleasure that he can't resist telling lies of all sizes.

Naturally, Cain tries to tell stories unlikely to be subjected to "fact checking," as it is called in the worlds of publishing and journalism. Often he won't begin sharing his fib with someone until assured that the "information" will be kept in the strictest confidence.

Cain may ask you to keep a story confidential, but he doesn't really mean it. On the contrary, he is usually telling a story to smear or undermine someone he dislikes, and he *wants* Abel to spread the lie as a rumor, which makes it more lethal and more credible because people assume that Abel, or someone Abel trusts (probably a reliable, disinterested person), is the source of the story. Cain simply doesn't want Abel to identify him as the author of the lie.

CASE STUDY 30

Late at night, after a long, long day, a well-established business consultant—an expert in corporate image and a Cain to the core—and a friend sat drinking at a hotel bar. In a moment of rare candor (brought on by one too many scotch and sodas), the consultant told his friend, "One secret in this business is this: Always be absolutely truthful and accurate with reporters, so that you can get away with lying to them when you have to.

"Let's say your own client is involved in some kind of controversy. Doesn't matter what. And you want to change the story. So, you call in a reporter and pass on some kind of rumor about some other company. You tell him it comes from a solid source.

"Chances are the reporter will go after the rumor because he knows that you're credible. Maybe he'll find something, maybe not. But there's always a chance he'll come across some dirt because almost any company is involved in something that could be controversial. It might have nothing to do with the original rumor you passed on, but it might still distract attention away from your guys and onto some other guys.

"But remember this: Always make certain that you're 'off the record'; or give it 'not for attribution,' or 'on deep background.' That way it can't be attributed to you."

What are the pertinent lessons in all of this?

First, don't agree to grant Cain blanket immunity by promising to keep confidential whatever he is about to tell you. Such a promise makes you complicit in his lie, complicit in what you should immediately suspect is privileged and possibly inaccurate information about someone else. You will be agreeing to remain quiet about the maligning of an innocent person. Is that worth satisfying your curiosity? What if you were slandered and a supposed friend of yours agreed to keep quiet about it? How would you feel about it?

Second, if Cain tells you about some "rumor" (a euphemism for "slander," but "rumor" is a word Cain frequently wields to entice you into passing on information), don't play his game. Don't share the story with others in your organization. It may be juicy, amusing, and fraught with all kinds of policy and/or personnel ramifications, but it might also be untrue and malevolent; it may be character assassination. Do you want to pass on a story that ruins someone's reputation—only to learn later that it's the big lie Cain wanted circulated? What then would you do? Take responsibility for spreading the false rumor? Apologize to the victim? What good would your apology do? The damage would already be done, and you would be responsible for the fallout, at least in part. Too often, "I'm sorry" is a substitute for doing the right thing in the first place. What other people want is for you not to do what you're now sorry for doing.

Sometimes Cain will unleash a blizzard of lies. In an *Esquire* article about Joseph R. McCarthy, the 1950s senator who slandered some innocent people by accusing them of associating with communists, Richard H. Rovere wrote, "McCarthy invented the Multiple Lie—the lie with so many tiny gears and fragile connecting rods that reason exhausted itself in the effort to combat it."

Cain often resorts to the multiple lie not only because it's more difficult for an adversary to respond to a series of detailed accusations, but also because Cain will occasionally be caught telling contradictory lies and will concoct new lies to cover and reconcile his old ones. Strangely enough, sometimes his explanations and excuses are so convoluted that his superiors and associates will suspend their disbelief or choose to ignore his lies because it's too mentally and emotionally taxing to cope with the tangled web of deceit, because they simply don't have the time to check everything out, or because they, themselves, might be humiliated by their own gullibility.

CASE STUDY 31

Kip McMaster was in his early thirties and was a young man in a hurry. He had political ambitions and proudly introduced himself as Judge McMaster, a state judge in Minnesota. His business cards highlighted his title, as did his stationery.

When his party's candidate was elected governor, Judge McMaster decided to become involved with the committee planning the new governor's inaugural events. He figured that it was an opportunity to meet and get to know some of the key players in the new administration, and who knew where that might lead?

Judge McMaster approached his old high school and explained that he had arranged with the inaugural committee to create an all-expenses-paid Governor's Scholars Program. Six outstanding students from a given high school would be chosen to work with the inaugural committee. Afterward, the students would submit papers describing what they had done and what they had learned from their experience.

Because he was the head of the program, he was able to designate his own high school as the participating school.

The six lucky students were selected by the school—they were the top of their class academically and in community and extracurricular activities. Judge McMaster met with them to describe the program and what they would be doing. He told them that they would be spending a week working with the inaugural committee, but it wasn't going to be all work; they would also be attending some of the social and entertainment events planned for the inaugural, so they should be certain to bring along formal dress clothes.

When the students arrived in the state capital, Judge McMaster met them and drove them in a van to a one-room unfurnished apartment. He explained that the inaugural committee had mixed up their hotel reservations, and it would take another day to untangle the confusion. In the meantime, he had convinced a friend to provide them with a free room for the night. He apologized for the rough accommodations and promised to take them out to a good restaurant for dinner that evening, which he did. When the check arrived, he told the students, "Now this is a great chance for you to learn how to divide up a check. It's a great lesson for real life, where you'll have to be doing this all the time in business or whatever you end up doing. Now go ahead, and each of you pay your share, including tip. I'll be back in a minute. I have to congratulate the chef on this fine meal."

After dinner, he took the students food shopping. They assumed he would foot the bill, but he again explained that they should each pay for what they bought—another "life experience." Back at the empty apartment, the students asked Judge McMaster for a coffee machine so they could at least make coffee for breakfast. He told them he would bring them one in the morning, but when he arrived, he had no coffee machine. "It has mold in it," he explained, "and I'm afraid if you use it, you might get sick. I'm a judge, and I know how easy it is to sue people these days."

Two days passed, and the students had done nothing except sleep on the floor and eat potato chips. On the third day, when they complained to Judge McMaster, he bundled them into his van and drove them to the scheduling office of the inaugural committee. There, no one had heard of the Governor's Scholars Program. "I can't believe this," an exasperated Judge McMaster said. "How incompetent can this new administration be?" The scheduling office quickly agreed to find positions for the students, who were set to work doing menial tasks.

After a third night of potato chips, sleeping on the bare floor of the unfurnished apartment, and no social or entertainment events of any kind, the students began calling home and complaining to their parents, who, in turn, called school officials to find out just what was going on.

The principal of the school called Judge McMaster, who was quick to apologize for the "incompetence" of the inaugural bureaucracy. He promised that suitable accommodations would be provided "even if I have to take this to the Governor himself."

One suspicious parent began looking into Judge McMaster's background and could find no judge of that name listed by the state. The parent relayed this information to his son, who confronted Judge McMaster. "I don't know what your father has been looking at," the judge insisted, "but I am a judge." When the boy demanded to see some proof, Judge McMaster handed him a license reading "Justice of the Peace."

"That's not a judge," the boy said.

"Let's look at the dictionary," the judge said. He pointed to the definition of "justice of the peace," which included the word "magistrate." Under "magistrate," the dictionary read, "a minor judicial official."

In the meantime, the school, afraid for its own responsibility in the matter, began investigating the judge's background. They were surprised to find no picture of him in the yearbook published the year he graduated. Again, the principal called the "judge," who explained, "I never got around to having a graduation picture taken when I was here. My family was poor, and we couldn't afford a formal picture. I was embarrassed to hand in an informal snapshot." The principal reluctantly accepted the explanation; what he really wanted to do was get away from this mess. It could cause him nothing but trouble.

After the fourth day of the "program," the "judge" disappeared. The inaugural committee, afraid of scandal during the governor's celebrations, washed their hands of the students and told them not to report again for work. The students paid their way home, having truly, in the "judge's" own words, had a "real life" experience. When they returned to school, the school officials persuaded them to let the matter drop. It wouldn't do good for anyone to pursue the matter.

Had they pursued it, they would have learned that Judge McMaster wasn't really a judge, he had never attended the high school (he chose it because it was located in an affluent and prestigious suburb), there was no such thing as a Governor's Scholars Program, no jobs had been arranged at the inaugural committee (the "judge" had never even spoken to the committee about the "program"), there never were any hotel accommodations, and there were no tickets to any of the inaugural events.

In multiple-lie cases like this, people might well figure that it is easier to hope for the best, namely, that Cain will just go away or at least stop his lying. Also, part of Cain's strength lies in the fact that most Abels find confrontation embarrassing and awkward. Once a liar vehemently denies lying, what can Abel do? He would have to repeat the accusation with prosecutorial aggressiveness. Most people are just plain too nice to do that.

When *should* Abel be that aggressive? It depends on the exact situation, on the particular Cain, on the other people involved. But one thing Abel should *not* do is fall for the multiple lie in the first place. Recognize it for what it is: either an attempt to throw up a smoke screen to hide other lies, or an attempt to overwhelm someone with so many lies that he can't convincingly rebut them all.

Skepticism is the best attitude to have regarding anything Cain says—advice aptly expressed in a note from a headmaster to parents: "If you promise not to believe everything your child says happens at this school, I'll promise not to believe everything he says happens at home."

21. BE WARY OF A "CHANGE OF HEART"

George Burns once quipped, "Acting is all about sincerity. If you can fake that, you've got it made." And for Cain, a "change of heart" is indeed an act.

Cain feigns sincerity and often seems devout in his convictions. But to Cain nothing is sacred; not religion, not family, not love. Kindness is a weakness in Cain's view. He considers politeness, courtesy, loyalty as old-fashioned affectations, sometimes useful as rhetorical ploys, but irrelevant, even corny, in the real world of cutthroat competition.

In Cain's quest to discover the "hot button issues" that turn people on and off (so he can press these buttons to his advantage when it's expedient), he quickly concludes that nothing succeeds like the appearance of sincerity. He's sincere all right—about getting his way.

This is not to say that Cain always lies. On occasion, he may calculate that candor and truthfulness are an effective tactic. If it suits his aim of winning Abel's trust and support, he will confess past sins or tell a sob story about his life to gain sympathy. When Abel hears this, he is inclined to be understanding, out of compassion . . . and relief. If Cain actually has a heart, if he's just misunderstood, it gives Abel hope that

Cain may cease to be a threat. But earth to Abel: Just because Cain admits to having certain problems doesn't mean that he sincerely regrets his selfishness. It doesn't mean he intends to change his ways.

22. LEAVE PSYCHOANALYSIS TO THE PROFESSIONALS

It's practically a cliché in TV sitcoms, soap operas, and prime-time dramas for one character to promise another character that he or she is "there for you," is sympathetic "in case you need someone who's been there," and is willing to listen "if you want to air it all out." Almost inevitably this prompts the distraught character to break down, spill his guts, and confess everything.

In nontelevision life, this kind of amateur therapy can be harmful to a person in distress. Even the most thoughtful, would-be shrink can lead a troubled friend astray by asking the wrong questions, by suggesting the wrong options, or by evincing worry at the wrong moments. Effective psychotherapy requires years of education, training, and experience. Serious personal problems can only be remedied with careful analysis, astute insight, accurate diagnosis, and sound advice.

This is not to say that well-meaning people shouldn't encourage friends and lend a sympathetic ear. But, what if you're the "patient"? Can you be certain that the person offering to listen is truly a friend? As a general rule, if you have the slightest doubt about a "confidant," do not disclose any embarrassing secrets to him or her. It could come back to haunt you later.

Abel is much more likely than Cain to make the mistake of opening up and divulging too much to someone untrustworthy.

Why?

First, Abel is inclined to think that trusting someone is, in and of itself, a step forward into a more hopeful future. To Cain, such blind faith is like trying to skate across quicksand. He doesn't trust anyone with his innermost secrets.

Second, Abel feels guilty if he refuses to share his thoughts when asked. Guilty of what? Of rudeness for rejecting a kind gesture. By contrast, Cain would be insulted by the presumptuous suggestion that something is wrong with him, and he would be instantly suspicious about the motives of anyone inquiring about his insecurities.

Third, Abel tends to think that he can deal better with a problem if he understands it clearly; sharing thoughts with a friend might be useful. Cain believes that most problems troubling him are someone else's fault. He just needs to get more power, money, or revenge in order to set matters right.

The main difference between the two of them, then, is this: Abel is more willing than Cain to open up. Cain feigns empathy to seduce others into baring their souls and revealing their fears and regrets, so he can use this information if it ever proves advantageous.

Cain might try to manipulate you, make you feel awkward, unless you share personal secrets with him. "Don't you trust me?" he might ask, and in order to prove that you trust him, you have to tell him what he wants to hear. But stop and think. Would a genuinely trustworthy person do this? An honorable person wouldn't press you to prove anything.

Cain can even pressure you with silence. Good reporters know that most people are uncomfortable with silence, and if you ask a question and then simply let a person talk without saying anything yourself, they will often reveal much more than what was asked for in the first place. They will first answer the question, but when the reporter then remains quiet, seeming as if he is waiting for more, the person starts talking again. About what? Well, since he has already answered the question asked, he is likely to branch off into other matters.

Don't fall for the listening game. If you have deep, dark secrets or wild, woolly ambitions or big, bad worries, keep them to yourself. Put your trust only in true-blue friends or a professional therapist. Don't take the risk of trusting a Cain, or, just as bad, trusting an Abel who might make the mistake of trusting a Cain with information about you.

But what if you have already made the mistake of confiding in Cain, or what if you let slip information to a supposed friend who in turn passed it on to Cain?

To begin with, be alert—anticipate the very real possibility that

Cain might use the information against you, directly or indirectly. Directly, he can "yank your chain," threatening to expose your secret if you don't go along with some scheme of his. In other words, he might blackmail you. But don't expect him to be blatant about it. Cain is likely to do this with subtlety. He might allude to your secret in the same conversation where he asks for a favor or proposes some scheme, implying that the two things are linked. Or, he might treat the matter humorously, as if it's just a sly dig unrelated to what he's really after. For example, if Cain knows you have a drinking problem, and now wants you to slip him a confidential document for some purpose, he might say, "Look, you know I'm good at keeping things quiet—like your secret affair with Jim Beam. You know I'll never say anything. We can trust each other."

But you *can't* trust Cain. In the example just given, you should refuse to cooperate and consider reporting the matter to higher-ups. Giving in to Cain's blackmail would only make your life more miserable. Once Cain discovers your weakness, he will continue asking for favors; he will ask for more and more, and he will never stop asking.

Given Abel's mind-set, it's easy for Cain to play the role of volunteer therapist, dispensing free analysis of Abel's anxieties, faults, and prejudices. (Of course, this is absurd. Cain is the one who clearly needs therapy.)

Why does Cain play the psychotherapist game? Because it enables him to plant seeds of self-doubt in the minds of people. Insecure people are more easily manipulated, and many people are insecure about their own abilities and, consequently, their job security. Think back to when we discussed Cain's "mind games." In asking a subordinate, "You like your job, don't you?" he is testing to determine a person's fear and vulnerability to a certain kind of pressure. Once he identifies this or any other weakness, he can use it to manipulate others for his own purposes. This information is just as useful to him if it comes from your voluntary self-confession instead of his threats.

If you fall for Cain's trick of "concerned listening," don't compound the error by tumbling for his follow-up trick: self-serving, smooth-talking psychotherapy. If Cain is trying to "help" you by exploring your foibles and woes, ask to see his professional therapist credentials. Plato declared, "The unexamined life is not worth living," but it is up to *you* to be introspective. Don't allow fakers to psych you out.

23. WATCH OUT WHO YOU PARTY WITH

It's best to avoid becoming involved with Cain socially. It's far better for him to consider you a snob than an ally because he has, or will eventually have, a reputation for abusing decent people, and that reputation could rub off on you. Some people might suspect that you condone his misconduct, or worse, that you play an active part in it. This is guilt by association (which usually connotes the unfair tainting of innocent people), but if you "hang out" with Cain, you can unwittingly help him in the status-seeking schmoozing that enables him to do some of his dirty work—rumormongering, ego-massaging, "opposition research." Cain isn't out just for a good time. He's looking for weaknesses, sniffing out inside information, maneuvering for gainful advantage.

Socializing is a big part of Cain's standard operating procedure. It's not that he finds people fascinating; it's that he finds them so much more vulnerable in a social setting, so much more inclined to gab about personal affairs and business antics. This is the kind of information he diligently pursues. It's his working capital, the stuff that makes dreams (or in Cain's case, schemes) come true.

Very few of us think we are the kind of person to "spill the beans" at a social event. A few drinks would never put us "under the influence," and we would never succumb to any of the other perils of the "party hearty" crowd. But memory can be self-serving, especially if we can't even remember the morning after what we said the night before. But Cain will remember. He might be intoxicated, but he's taking mental notes, on high alert for the pratfalls and frailties of others.

Finally, and this may be the most telling reason to avoid partying with Cain, you should understand that, above all else, he wants to put you in a compromising position. If he can wink at you the following day as if he now knows the real you; if he can hint to other people that you told him things that were very revealing, even if you didn't; if he believes that you are now someone he can readily gossip with, or share schemes with, or ridicule colleagues with, you are going to play a more prominent role in his mind and in his plans. You can always refuse his overtures, but he'll be all the more embittered when you do. Be aware that socializing with Cain makes you vulnerable to him, and he's going to view you as being just as much on the make as he is. You may not have said or done a single thing to encourage his attitude, but it takes precious little for him to draw such conclusions because they help him justify and rationalize his own selfishness.

Keeping in mind Cain's real purpose, is your participation in his socializing really so innocent?

24. DON'T BE TRAPPED BY THE TRAPPINGS OF SUCCESS

To make sure that you aren't duped by Cain, the con artist, ask yourself the following questions.

- Are you impressed by spacious offices, luxury cars, elegant furnishings, and expensive clothes?
- Are you intimidated, at least a little, by powerful executives who are so busy juggling cell-phone calls, urgent requests for appointments, and high-level meetings that they can barely focus on you and your business?
- Are you apt to judge someone's status by the perks they enjoy, their job title, and their social connections?

If you're honest with yourself, you probably answered yes to all of the above. Unless you have a Zen-like detachment from all things material, or are extremely unobservant about your surroundings, you draw inferences about someone's social and business standing from the so-called trappings of success.

In an ideal world, this might not be the case; we would be so wrapped up in doing creative or charitable work that we would never invest ourselves in such worldly things, nor even take note of them. But this is the *real* world, and Cain knows it. As we've discussed, he wants all the status, perks, and intimidating advantages that he can get because, like any con artist, he knows that the trappings of success can beget even more success. In other words, while it may be tragically unfair, it's often true that the rich get richer while the poor get poorer.

Consider Harvard University. It is the world's second-wealthiest not-for-profit institution, after the Roman Catholic Church, and yet its alumni continue to give hundreds of millions more to it every year. Does Harvard need the money? Not according to any normal definition of "need." Many countries in the world have less in their treasuries. Nonetheless, people like to be part of a great success story, and so the alumni continue to give generously.

Cain understands this, and, therefore, spends plenty of time, energy, and capital acquiring the trappings of success. This may sound perfectly sensible, given that an impressive facade is apparently part of the "cost of doing business" in a competitive world. But beware. Cain will aggressively concoct a fraudulent image of success. He will use the trappings of success to entrap people, taking advantage of their faith to dupe them. He may create phony business cards or stationery for companies that exist only on paper. Cain may drop the names of influential people—people he's never met. In his office, he may have the cushiest carpeting, the tallest chair, and the most polished desk. He may have a prestigious office address, and yet be running out of money, but he will still be eager to take your money before filing for bankruptcy.

Do not trust your "lying eyes." The "trappings of success" are designed to impress prospective customers, investors, or anyone who might be useful to Cain. Beneath these surface appearances, the truth may be very different. To avoid being seduced by the illusion of success, do some basic research. Find out if the people who want your money or want you to work for them are what they purport to be. Do they have a history of performance? Do they have a reputation for integrity? What do public records reveal about them? What do their competitors say about them? Are they trying to impress you, or are they trying to reason with you? If they try to pressure you for an immediate acceptance of any proposition, solely on the basis of apparent success, alarm bells should go off inside your head.

25. DON'T PLAY THE BLAME GAME

Economists explain market fluctuations in terms of "supply and demand." Coaches and athletes evaluate every possible play in terms of "win or lose." Cain has a similar black-or-white view of his work: He analyzes every work situation in terms of blame and credit. As an organization man, he's far less concerned with innovation, employee morale, and product quality than with whether he's rising or falling measured by power, prestige, perks and money. Consequently, he's always focused on who gets the credit for any accomplishment and who is blamed for any fumble.

In his 1987 book, *How to Work for a Jerk,* Robert M. Hochheiser wrote that many so-called business experts must subscribe to "the tooth fairy of business management" because they assume that all employees actually care about their organization; that all conflicts are nothing more than honest differences of opinion; and that better communication will automatically improve working relationships. If Cain is at work in an organization, these assumptions aren't just naive, they're laughably wrong. He cares only about himself, he enjoys getting others in trouble, and he uses communication to grab credit and assign blame, not to promote cooperation.

What then do you do when Cain unfairly tries to cast blame or brazenly steal credit?

1. Accept the unpleasant fact that he will sometimes get away with credit theft and blame deflection. If you spend too much of your time keeping an eye on him—scrutinizing his claims, double-checking everything he says, trying to anticipate his every move—you will end up neglecting your own duties, making yourself his primary target, and earning a reputation as a paranoid, contentious nitpicker. Remember Hippocrates' rule for physicians: "First, do no harm." Take his advice, and do no harm

to yourself. Cain might eventually be caught stealing credit or falsely affixing blame, but many a Cain manages to hang on even under a constant cloud of suspicion. When exposed, Cain won't resign. He has no sense of honor and can live with a loss of dignity. To Cain, those are antiquated concepts anyway. (The original Cain never confessed to his crime. When the Lord asked Cain: "Where is Abel, thy brother?" he replied: "I know not; am I my brother's keeper?") So, while hoping that Cain does himself in, what can you do to protect yourself from becoming the victim of his blame game or his credit fraud?

2. To avoid being blind-sided by Cain, try to anticipate the "ricochet" of blame if things go wrong. Where will the blame begin, and how might it bounce around? Who will accept the blame and who will pass it on, and to whom? If your project involves even a slight risk, don't be so blindly optimistic about the outcome that you overlook the consequences of what might happen if things go awry.

3. To protect yourself from undeserved blame, document your work. Keep time-sensitive records of what you've done. Use memos and e-mail to inform and update your associates about what you've accomplished. In other words, verify your record and your innocence.

4. If you have reason to believe that Cain is misrepresenting your work to others—either unfairly casting blame on you or taking credit that is rightfully yours—send a factual report to these people. In the report, don't whine about Cain. If your version is accurate and convincing, Cain will be discredited to some extent without your hurling personal accusations that make you sound anxious, bitter, or defensive.

5. If Cain has managed to unjustly blame you for something and put you on the spot, but you can't prove that he's the culprit, don't waste time fuming about it. Remember, Cain can hurt you by getting under your skin. If you've been stewing about the unfairness of it all, you're more likely to explode when the issue is

raised. Don't assume that your spontaneous, sputtered indignation will "prove" your innocence. Excessive protestations can seem suspicious, and people may wonder: Why do you sound so defensive if you're totally innocent? Instead, think calmly. Carefully consider what you'll say in explanation, if asked. Most important, try to view your case from the viewpoint of those who will be judging you. If you're able to do that, you may be surprised to discover that you can defuse the situation with fact and tact, and perhaps with humor. Outrage—loss of control—is rarely effective. If you try to protect your reputation by lashing out in anger, you will end up undermining your reputation for being steady and rational.

6. Realize that you can't beat Cain at the blame game or the credit fraud game. You *can* beat him at the respect and leadership game. Play by the rules of this game—share credit, and take responsibility when things go wrong—and you win. People respond positively to someone willing to give credit where credit is due, and, if mistakes are made, accept responsibility. Try to be patient and have faith in the fact that Cain's tactics may be effective in the short term but are often self-defeating in the long run.

26. DON'T IGNORE OFFICE POLITICS

Dan Payne, a media consultant, is a past practitioner of politics from the grassroots level on up to federal campaigns, yet he asserts, "Politics in a big corporation, college, or even charity can be as ruthless and filled with intrigue as the internal processes of any political campaign."

What constitutes "office politics"? Quite simply, it is anything that influences the decision-making process about who gets what, when, where, why, and how . . . whether it be a promotion, pay raise, company car, a free parking place, a new job title, added responsibilities, preferred customers, a bigger office, more support staff, greater autonomy, a larger budget, and so on.

In an ideal world, all of the perks and power decisions would be based on merit, or in some cases, seniority or financial need. But in the real world, the thing we call office politics often determines the way decisions are made: people helping other people because of loyalty, favors, personality, promises, threats, expediency, fear, resentment, admiration, or greed. And it is usually quite subjective. If someone gets a promotion, he feels that he "earned it"; the rival who lost out may call it "typical office politics."

Cain has a cynical view of internal decision-making. He considers it all politics all the time, and views every creature in the organizational jungle in terms of whether they are useful to him. Merit, talent, and competence are irrelevant. The criterion that guides him is simple: Can a person or situation help him acquire power, money, or status? Can someone help him get even with his enemies?

Like a "black hole" that consumes anything that comes near it, this self-centered view can suck all the energy out of a team-oriented staff. Whenever someone is pumping poisonous suspicion and cynicism into the office atmosphere, the spirit of the workplace changes dramatically. The old adage that "one rotten apple can spoil the whole barrel" is a cliché because, like all clichés, it is so often proven true.

How can you counteract Cain's political gambits? Begin by realizing that "office politics" is an unavoidable reality. Decision-making in any organization will never be based on merit alone. Earth is not Vulcan, Mr. Spock's planet, where logic and reason control all things. The issue then becomes, what kind of office politics will prevail? If Cain decides the answer to this question, you're not going to be happy with the result. It will be the politics of the carnivore, the law of the jungle, and if you don't go along with Cain, your days will be numbered.

But it doesn't have to be this way. Office politics doesn't have to be the nasty, foolish game that the term suggests. "Politics" also implies a system where compromise allows people to put aside differences and get things done constructively. "Politics" is diplomacy for peacemaking. "Politics" is taking turns when there is no fairer way to decide who should receive an honor. "Politics" is airing disagreements so that a synthesis of opinion or of new ideas can be shaped. So, don't ignore or reject office politics as unworthy. If you do, you will allow Cain to control it. Instead, resolve to be a positive, constructive participant in it. You can't win a contest if you refuse to compete in it.

27. CULTIVATE ALLIES

Abel is likely to operate on his own, confident that right makes might and good work will be rewarded. If only it were so easy. Cain knows that the biggest challenge in office politics is to cultivate support for your interests.

Who is right? Is the conscious, deliberate recruiting of allies "calculating, self-serving, and shrewd," or is it a practical necessity for competing and succeeding in the real world?

The answer depends on how you go about it—in a fair, honest way, or in Cain's way. Since Cain doesn't trust others, suspecting that their ambitions are much like his own, he tries to compel support by preying on people's weaknesses, vices, and fears. He prefers this negative approach because he enjoys the sense of superiority and sadistic thrill it gives him, and, equally, because he believes it is a more reliable way to control others. If he can hold them hostage by threatening to fire, demote, or humiliate them, he feels more assured of their support in any situation.

Abel cannot, would not, should not lower himself to Cain's level, but at the same time, Abel shouldn't ignore what people might do if conflict arises. If Abel concentrates exclusively on his work, while around him a problem is becoming a crisis and people are choosing up sides, he may discover that Cain has already persuaded many or even most others to join his alliance. The deck may be stacked. Abel can always demand a new deal, but it's probably too late.

CASE STUDY 32

Drew was the executive director of a small research foundation that had been founded and funded by a wealthy businessman. The businessman's brother, who had no real position or role in the foundation's activities, nonetheless had strong opinions about how the operation should function. He was also a man who never forgot or forgave any kind of slight, no matter how small.

The brother would telephone Drew five or six times a day with suggestions of one kind or another. Each time, he would take ten to fifteen minutes of Drew's time as the brother rambled on about his newest inspiration.

After several weeks of these interruptions, Drew told his administrative assistant to tell the brother that Drew had gone out and wasn't available.

Unfortunately for Drew, the brother had an ally on the foundation's staff, a "spy" who regularly reported back to him about what was going on in the office. When the brother learned that Drew had lied to him about being absent, he was furious . . . and was determined from that moment to get rid of Drew.

The brother began by telling the wife of the man who had founded and funded the foundation that Drew often ridiculed her looks and intelligence to members of the staff, and the brother's ally confirmed this to the wife. Of course, it was a lie, but in her anger, the wife never checked. Then the brother began treating various staff members to lunch, where he would "confide" in them.

"Drew told me he thinks you're not totally loyal, and he may have to let you go."

"Drew says you've been taking too much sick time. He's planning to crack down. You better watch your back."

"Drew thinks you're a flake. He actually said that the other day. I didn't think it was very nice, and I told him so."

None of this was true, but they all believed it anyway. And, of course, they thought kindly of the "friend" who had warned them about what was "going on behind their backs" at the office.

Drew eventually learned about the brother's conspiracy,

but he chose to ignore it. He had the trust and confidence of the founder, and that's all he needed. Besides, he had real work to do and real things to worry about.

But the founder's relationship with Drew was being slowly undermined by the constant stream of complaints and criticism coming not only from the staff, but from his wife. Drew was becoming more trouble than he was worth, a problem easily solved when the founder called Drew in and fired him.

But, who could the founder trust to run the operation? Why, his brother, of course. After all, most of the staff and his own wife thought highly of him.

The Lesson: Do some coalition-building in advance. If you sense distant rumbles of trouble from Cain concerning your job or your project, explain to the people in your organization what you want to accomplish and why—even if some of them are not directly involved. Get the truth out. You may worry that you're wasting time—yours and theirs—but often in the process of explaining and defending your work, you will discover better ways to accomplish and promote it.

If you are confident that truth is on your side and that Cain would have to grossly misrepresent your views to defeat your position, don't wait for a showdown at the O.K. Corral. That plays into Cain's hands. He prefers an ambush and is ever alert for the opportunistic, expedient way of doing things. While you are proceeding blithely along, focusing on your own work, he's approaching people behind your back. Anticipate this, and seek out allies ahead of time. Win their backing. Once you build a coalition of support, you will significantly lessen the chance that Cain will attack, and if he does, he will end up undermining his own credibility.

CHAPTER 17

◆ ◆ ◆

Don't Jump to Conclusions

After considering all this advice and the views of the therapists in Chapter 14, it's time for a one-question pop quiz.

Is Cain's unethical nature the result of:

a. poor parenting?
b. abuse by family members?
c. pressure from peers?
d. lack of moral instruction?
e. an overly competitive social system?
f. all of these factors?

The correct answer is: It all depends on the individual Cain.

Even if we were talking about a real-life Cain, rather than generalizing about a hypothetical one, professional therapists would evaluate him in different ways, come to different conclusions, and suggest different kinds of treatment for him . . . assuming that they would accept him as a patient in the first place.

But our aim is to understand how to *cope* with a Cain. It doesn't matter whether Cain is the way he is as a result of nature or nurture, genetic makeup or peer pressure, or having been born when the stars and planets were strangely aligned. Because you're not going to change him. You're not going to be able to arrange an "intervention" where his family, business associates, and old acquaintances confront him (in the spirit of "tough love") about his selfish ways, break down his resistance with passionate testimony, and force him to understand that he must reform himself. It's not going to happen, except in your dreams.

Nonetheless, understanding Cain's driven, egocentric nature can help you to better deal with him. As one of the therapists pointed out, knowing that Cain might be reenacting some kind of abuse from his own past can help you control your own anger and desire for revenge. Cain "wins" if his actions force you into behaving like him. If you can restrain yourself and avoid victimizing someone else, you can break the cycle of Cain's unethical maneuvering and exploitation, and, in that way, diminish Cain's influence on the world; at least on your personal world. This may sound like small consolation if Cain is making your life miserable. But step back from your resentment and fear: You'll be better able to see clearly and figure out how to improve your situation.

Cain isn't easy to diagnose, and he's not easy to identify. He's not a cartoon villain, wearing a black cape, cursing with a Transylvanian accent, and kicking dogs as he goose-steps down the street. Still, you should be able to recognize a Cain.

Let's try another one-question pop quiz. Can you identify the following Cain, as described by his nemesis?

He is a man of good birth and excellent education . . . and had, to all appearances, a most brilliant career before him. But the man had hereditary tendencies of the most diabolical kind. A criminal strain ran in his blood. . . . He sits motionless, like a spider in the center of its web, but that web has a thousand radiations, and he knows well every quiver of each of them. He does little himself. He only plans. But his agents are numerous and splendidly organized. . . . He is the Napoleon of crime . . .

If you recognized Sherlock Holmes' description of Professor Moriarty, you should audition for *Jeopardy!* and use your winnings to move far away from the Cain whose nasty nature motivated you to buy this book.

The description of Moriarty, the quintessential criminal mastermind, comes from Sir Arthur Conan Doyle's story, "The Final Problem." The fans of Sherlock Holmes were fascinated by the thought that a singular diabolical man was "the organizer of half that is evil and of nearly all that is undetected in this great city." Perhaps the more mundane idea that crime is the outgrowth of millions of minds, an epidemic of single-self corruption, was too unsettling.

Human nature has not changed much in the one hundred years since Conan Doyle created Moriarty. Many people still prefer to believe that "half that is evil and of nearly all that is undetected" can be traced to criminal conspiracies if only we had a brilliant, daring sleuth to do the dangerous investigative undercover work.

But as Sherlock Holmes himself observed, "Life is infinitely stranger than anything which the mind of man could invent." And what could be stranger than the reality of many different kinds of corrupt individuals, with many different backgrounds, and many different reasons for their being the way they are?

Life is not only infinitely strange but strangely infinite, because every human being is unique. E. M. Forster, the English writer, said there are two kinds of people in the world: those who say there are two kinds of people in the world and those who don't say that. The thesis of this book is not that there are only two kinds of people (Cains and Abels), but rather, that we all have two forces playing tug-of-war inside of us, corrupting temptations versus innate conscience, and that in a relatively small number of people corruption has won out. We repeat: *In a relatively small number of people* the corrupt side has won out.

Therefore, we underscore this important advice: Don't make the mistake of thinking that everyone who uses Cain tactics is necessarily a Cain.

There are several reasons why it is wrong to make snap judgments about people.

1. You could easily be wrong.

Perhaps what you've heard about the supposed Cain is untrue or has been taken out of context and distorted. Or perhaps what the alleged Cain did is an aberration caused by extraordinary circumstances. He may regret his behavior and want to make up for the pain he caused by setting things right. In any case, it is unwise to rush to judgment and then make matters worse by sharing your unfair opinion with other people.

2. **If you rashly conclude that your troubles are caused by a Cain, you are less likely to look in the mirror and recognize your own faults.**

   It's easy to blame an adversary for one's own lack of success; it's much harder to face the truth that one's own laziness, lack of talent, or personality might be the real cause of failure. If you don't recognize and accept your own shortcomings you are unlikely to overcome them.

3. **If you misidentify someone as a Cain and assume that he's a hopeless case, you will miss the opportunity to help change his conduct.**

   Once you decide someone is a Cain, you will tend to avoid him. Certainly, you won't risk confronting him. But if you are mistaken and the person is "guilty" of simple expediency or foolishness, you will have passed up the chance to redirect his behavior with constructive advice, or incentives, or new rules, or encouragement, or embarrassment, or other "management" methods.

It's worthwhile examining each of these in greater depth because you can do real harm to your own reputation and livelihood by falling into these traps.

◆ *YOU COULD EASILY BE WRONG.*

Consider this real-life example.

A young, single mother was hired by a communications firm through a temporary employment agency. Assigned as an assistant to a middle-aged, midlevel female manager, she was happy and grateful to get the position. She had two children to support and needed the income, and she appreciated the opportunity to acquire new skills that would make her more employable once the temp job ended.

At first, she got along well with her new boss, who often took her out to lunch, praised her work, and raised the possibility of hiring her on a permanent basis. Occasionally, her boss allowed her to reschedule her working hours in order to tend to an ailing parent.

But one day, viciously and without warning, the boss upbraided the temp for a small mistake, a reaction so out of proportion that the temp was stunned and extremely upset the rest of the day. The next morning, the boss appeared to be in fine spirits, seemingly oblivious to the blowup of the previous day. But in the weeks that followed, the boss was noticeably less friendly. She would chew out the temp in front of other employees, belittle her over trivial matters, and generally make her work life miserable.

Working relationships don't exist in a vacuum. In this case, the company was in the midst of a merger with a large conglomerate, and all of those in management felt a growing anxiety about keeping their jobs. The temp's boss was no exception. Apparently, she saw the temp as a threat to her position. Why? Because the temp had learned her boss's job so well that she was able to perform all of her boss's duties, and perform them well, whenever the boss was absent. The boss realized this and knew that many other people in her department realized it as well, which made her feel even more insecure. Worse yet, the temp had become quite popular in the firm and was now hoping for a permanent job with the company. What if the cost-conscious new regime came in and decided to fire the older, high-salaried middle manager and replace her with the younger, ambitious, and less expensive temp? The thought of that possibility drove the boss into fits of rage. To protect her own job and sanity, the manager fired the temp, and did so secretively at the end of a Friday, right before the Christmas holidays.

Was the manager a Cain? Or was she acting out of panic, desperately trying to hang on to her job?

Understandably, the temp was furious with her boss. Not only had she been frequently abused by a woman she had loyally served, she was rewarded by being fired. Despite her animosity, however, the temp kept a balanced view of what had occurred. The boss hadn't done a selfish, vicious thing because she enjoyed it. The fact was that she was unhappy with herself. From their lunches together, the temp knew that her boss was taking a prescription drug for manic depression, which explained some of her mood swings; she was a medicated, stressed out, insecure person. This condition, coupled with the fear of losing her job, obviously affected her entire attitude and outlook. The temp knew that her boss was in the process of self-destructing, alienating not only the temp but other people at work as well.

When the temp was told she was being let go, she appealed to higher-ranking executives in the company, who were furious that she had been treated so shabbily. They took her case to the president of the firm. In turn, the president reprimanded the temp's boss for firing a worker without fair notice, and arranged to have the temp re-hired in another department.

While the boss was certainly Cain-like in some respects, she wasn't truly a Cain. She was someone driven by a serious psychological problem and situational fear. It would have been easy for the temp to demonize her boss, but instead, the temp patiently sized up the situation and calmly presented her side of the story to others. She didn't make the mistake of assuming that her boss was a wicked schemer with tentacles reaching throughout the company. She kept everything in the proper perspective, and was able to think and act sensibly as a result, and she ended up doing better for herself and for her family.

◆ *IF YOU RASHLY CONCLUDE THAT YOUR TROUBLES ARE CAUSED BY A CAIN, YOU ARE LESS LIKELY TO LOOK IN THE MIRROR AND RECOGNIZE YOUR OWN FAULTS.*

In your daydreams, it's easy to make some adversary into a villain, with you playing the role of martyr or unsung hero. But daydreams are just that—daydreams. To fulfill your career dreams, you need to make sure that the problems you attribute to Cain are not of your own making.

You might resent someone else's success because it's a painful reminder of your own career stagnation. If that's the case, you have to resist the temptation to exaggerate your rival's insidious behavior. Before you conclude that another Cain has "gotten away with murder," ask yourself: "Is this just sour grapes on my part?" Has someone actually been unethically impeding your progress, or have you failed to do enough to advance yourself? If you put a little more effort into your job, would you be doing better? Montaigne, the father of the essay, put it bluntly: "If others excel you in knowledge, in charm, in strength, in fortune, you can blame external causes for it; but if you fall behind them in stoutness of spirit, you have only yourself to blame."

We all enjoy watching a fictional cross-examination on TV, where a villain is shrewdly unmasked and forced to face the truth. But *self-examination* is far more difficult to conduct successfully. Painful truths about ourselves are hard to face. We hide them from ourselves and are unlikely to force ourselves to think about them, let alone question our own motives, admit our fears, strip away our rationalizations, face our hypocrisy, and recognize the contradictions in our reasoning. Self-examination is so excruciating and complicated that people often need the help of a professional or spouse or mentor to get through it successfully.

Perhaps the following questions will help you determine whether you are looking to blame the wrong person for problems and botched opportunities. Try to answer each one as honestly as you can.

- Are you dedicating as much energy to pursuing your ambitions as the alleged Cain is spending on his?
- Do you consider yourself tactful and diplomatic?
- Are you jealous, envious, and resentful of people who succeed in competition with you?
- Do you pay much attention to the "politics" of a situation?
- Are you spending extra time—outside of your usual work—to develop new skills or talents?
- Are you patient with people who don't measure up to your standards?

- Do you try to build support for your ideas and projects by cultivating the backing of other people?
- Do you go out of your way to understand what motivates others?
- Do you spend time trying to anticipate what could go wrong in your work, and how you would defend your work against criticism?
- Do you enjoy your work?

These are very broad questions, and there are no perfectly correct answers. Much depends on how you interpret each question and how you view yourself. Still, if you answered most of these questions with a "no" or "not really" or anything other than "yes," chances are very good that your lack of success is less the result of a Cain holding you down than of your own attitudes holding you back.

Even if you yourself are responsible for your problems, the person you think is a Cain might still be a real Cain. If so, the question is how much effort should you spend coping with Cain, and how much time should you spend working to improve yourself? How much better off would you be if you:

- devote more energy to pursuing your ambitions
- be more tactful
- overcome your jealousy, envy, and resentment of others
- pay more attention to the "politics" of a difficult situation
- spend more time on developing new skills and latent talent
- be more patient with others
- cultivate the support of others for your ideas and projects
- go out of your way to understand and appreciate the motivations of others
- spend more time anticipating what could go wrong in your work and how to answer possible criticism of it
- learn to enjoy your work more, or perhaps find a new line of work

◆ *IF YOU MISIDENTIFY SOMEONE AS A CAIN AND ASSUME THAT HE'S A*
HOPELESS CASE, YOU WILL MISS THE OPPORTUNITY TO HELP CHANGE
HIS CONDUCT.

We are all imperfect. Most of us occasionally do things we regret
and might be ashamed of later. However, we are also the only crea-
tures, at least on this planet, who measure our actions against standards
of perfection. So, there is almost always some hope for improvement,
however marginal.

The president of Borg-Warner expressed this optimistic attitude in
1976 in his firm's policy manual for employees:

> I realize that business is conducted by people whose personal
> standards vary widely. However, at Borg-Warner, we tradition-
> ally seek to hire only people of high moral standards and, believ-
> ing we have done so, we trust you to maintain those standards in
> your service with us. Should there be any doubt about the moral-
> ity of any action you are considering on Borg-Warner's behalf,
> ask yourself these questions: Would I be willing to tell my family
> about the actions I am contemplating? Would I be willing to go
> before a community meeting, a Congressional hearing, or any
> public forum, to describe the action? In any case, if you would
> not be willing to do so, Borg-Warner would not want you to go
> ahead with the action on the assumption it would help the com-
> pany.

This is a useful guide for employee conduct and one way that a
modern firm will try to create a positive corporate culture. But what
can a company do about a Cain who considers "work ethics" an oxymoron?

As we have pointed out, there is little one can do to reform Cain's
nature or outlook. He's not going to be persuaded to change his ways
by guidelines in an employee manual. They are meaningless to him.
Cain considers codes of ethics something meant for *other* people, the
poor chumps who actually take such things seriously.

But again, what if the person you think is a Cain really isn't one? How do you determine if someone *is* or *isn't* a Cain? No employee manual or simple formula can answer this question.

"There are many personnel experts who will happily provide a statistically exact psychological profile of an effective sales person," explained Louis Dehmlow, former chairman of the National Association of Wholesaler-Distributors. "And they will determine for you, through tests and interviews, which of your job applicants best fits the description. The methodology they use, and the analysis they offer, could not seem more scientific or impressive. As employers, however, if we are to successfully motivate and inspire those same people, we have to go beyond the *science* of personnel sociology into the *art* of understanding them as unique individuals."

Science may soon be able to read a person's entire genetic code, and thus the likelihood that a person may or may not fall victim to a particular disease. But personal qualities are not easy to predict, and the lack of a conscience is undetectable. This doesn't mean that you shouldn't try to "read" people. But it does mean that you should be patient in letting people reveal themselves.

People who have had a lot of experience with Cains may become quite good at recognizing Cains. Also they may become cynical. Here is how a former assistant district attorney explained his perspective after years of prosecuting "low-life, career criminals":

"These guys would come in, smokin' and jokin', not a care in the world because they were confident they had beaten the system. They knew that witnesses weren't going to show or the police search was bad and knew that we wouldn't waste time trying to prosecute them. But, after a while, you get a long-term perspective in law enforcement: you know that what goes around comes around. You know they'll be back. Maybe they'll be caught in a stolen car or on surveillance video—something air-tight, rock-solid—and you will drop the bomb on 'em. Then they'll be sitting in the docket, this time with their heads down. The smirks are gone. They know they've lost, that it's over for them, that you've got them without an alibi. If you wait long enough, it'll happen. They'll get caught. Of course, in between, they can do a lot of damage, but that's another story. But when they fall, they fall hard. So, I learned to have the patience of Job."

There is a hint of understandable cynicism in the assistant district attorney's voice, but cynicism can be misleading. It can cause you to read someone incorrectly and judge him wrongly to be a Cain—someone to avoid because he's beyond help. This could be an unfortunate mistake. Why not take a small risk and try to steer someone onto the right path before concluding that he's hopeless? Obviously we're not referring to extreme cases (for example, vicious criminals), but rather to individuals who may be temporarily down on their luck, coping with a personal problem, or dealing with special pressures. These people may simply need some guidance and a helping hand.

There are plenty of management tools for guiding people into responsible behavior: incentives, penalties, strict supervision, psychological counseling, rules and regulations. Giving up on people without really giving them a chance to improve themselves can be *mis*management or just plain uncharitable.

Sometimes you have to be patient to catch a Cain. Other times, you have to be patient to avoid mistaking someone for a Cain. And still other times, you have to look in the mirror and say: wait a minute, Cain is not holding me back; I am.

⋄ ⋄ ⋄

CHAPTER 18

Words of Warning,
Words of Wisdom

Although we have used the Cain and Abel metaphor to illustrate how cunning often slays ability, remember that the competition between Cain and Abel is not a religious war between good and evil. Cain is not satanic, and Abel is not a saint. The two archetypes are meant to represent ordinary people working within the "normal" boundaries of today's business and political world. We have left the analysis of extremely aberrant personalities (murderous cheerleader moms, the Menendez brothers, the Unabomber) to the real experts—psychoanalysts and criminologists.

People who are 100 percent Cain or 100 percent Abel are very rare. In most of us, the two extremes wrestle for dominance. Robert Browning, the English poet, alluded to this internal struggle when he wrote, "When the fight begins within himself, a man's worth something." We are all imperfect, we are all capable of succumbing to temptation under some circumstances, yet it is this moral struggle inside us that determines our character. And it is our character that ultimately determines our destiny.

THE REAL WORLD

Whenever we have used the phrase "the real world," it has carried the connotation of "menacing" and "unpleasant." And that is what the real world of politics and business tends to become when a Cain is present. If the world were ordinarily loving, cooperative, and friendly, then the "real world" would refer to a wondrous place where people succeed to the degree that they use their skills industriously, in concert with others, in an honest way. Period. Unfortunately, this does not describe the typical workplace, even in the new millennium. No, the "real world" does not refer to utopia, but rather to an everyday environment where "real" can sometimes mean "unfair."

For Abel, this kind of unfairness—often caused by the machinations of Cain—should be the beginning of the story, not the end. It doesn't do Abel any good to feel sorry for himself, or to feel virtuous because he's unwilling to "cut corners" if Cain keeps winning out in the end. When dealing with Cain, Abel has to become smarter about the real world, not just smarter in taking tests or doing assigned work. Abel has to *act;* he has to do something to improve his own position and to make the world a fairer place.

The most important step in dealing with any problem is first to become aware of and accept the fact that one exists; the second step is understanding its precise nature so that a suitable remedy can be figured out.

The purpose of this book is to encourage greater awareness of Cain and foster an understanding of who he is and how he operates. As we have noted, forewarned is forearmed. And an Abel armed with a knowledge of Cain is more than a match for him. This is especially true because there are far more Abels than Cains, so Abel has the advantage of numbers. He can draw on the sympathy and support of the Abels around him in his conflict with Cain . . . so long as he uses his knowledge to anticipate Cain's ploys and thwart Cain's schemes.

For practical reasons, our analysis and advice assumes that Cain is already present in your workplace and probably causing you grief. If you're lucky and Cain-free at the moment, but you suspect one is applying for a position in your organization, you can do the obvious: Check his prior work experience by calling his references. Better yet, check with people at his previous place of employment whom he does *not* offer as references—colleagues, support staff, perhaps even vendors or clients—and try to get the full story. This kind of research may seem intrusive and impolite to a trusting (Read: "naive") Abel, but it should be a standard precaution before hiring anyone for a position of power and responsibility. After all, many people will be affected by any such decision. An applicant who is indignant about appropriate inquiries and reasonable fact-checking is probably afraid of what might be discovered.

THE MORAL OF THE STORY

Cain may be a lying, conniving backstabber, but, again, remember that we're not talking about pure evil. Indeed, because he is not totally malevolent he is all the more effective in getting his way.

"There are bad people who would be less dangerous if they were quite devoid of goodness," wrote François La Rochefoucauld, a seventeenth century French writer. He was absolutely right. A Cain who has a few redeeming qualities is far more dangerous than a Cain without any because he's not going to be shunned by society. He will be free to operate among the unsuspecting and vulnerable and will be able to exploit them more easily.

The chapter title promised a big WOW, "Words of Wisdom." What are they? And do they provide a happy ending to offset all these troubling Words of Warning?

Yes, if you take them to heart.

First, there is the consoling thought that Cain often ends up as a failure. Once someone earns a reputation as a liar, he no longer has the credibility and respect needed to rise in most organizations. Once someone is seen as sadistic and conniving, he no longer has the trust and support needed to be a true leader. Once someone reveals himself to be a backstabbing paranoid, he will have too many real enemies to prevail over the long run. His days will be numbered.

If this is the inevitable outcome for Cain, why do we bother to offer so much analysis and advice for dealing with these people? As you probably know by now, some of these Cains can get away with murder for a very long time and cause a lot of pain while they do. Some manage to get away with hurting good people all of their lives. They may have to relocate a lot, but they still manage.

Our purpose is not to delight in the downfall of Cain, even if he deserves it. Our aim is to help people successfully cope with Cain in the here and now.

In that spirit, the wisest advice concerns your own outlook. How should you view competition with Cain in the "real world"?

THE "REAL WORLD" IS INSIDE YOU

If you have an embittered view of life, if you view people with envy, if you have a cynical view of your work, if you have a pessimistic view of your own hopes for success, chances are, you are going to fail in competition with anyone—Cain included—because the world you envision will make you feel anxious, timid, and sluggish. Defeatism is self-fulfilling. But, if you love life, enjoy your work, accept adversity as a challenge, and tend to see the best in people, you probably will succeed in competition with anyone, including someone like Cain who refuses to play by the rules.

KEEP "WINNING" IN PERSPECTIVE

The value of having a positive outlook goes beyond winning in the workplace and achieving career goals. The real victory is in the day to day satisfaction that comes with feeling that you're living the right way for yourself and for others. This is a happiness that Cain will never know. Indeed, it is Cain's dissatisfaction with himself and his life that fosters his greed, envy, and bitterness. Regardless of how he fares in terms of money, power, and status, Cain will remain a scheming egotist and very few people will ever like, respect, or admire him.

APPRECIATE YOUR ENEMIES

Being philosophical about a person who makes your life miserable is easier said than done. Some people are capable of overcoming animosity toward others through generosity of spirit, some through sheer will power. Still others control their reactions through self-interested reason. "Pay attention to your enemies, for they are the first to discover your mistakes," observed Antisthenes of ancient Greece. We should be at least somewhat grateful for what adversaries teach us. We learn about our own weaknesses from them. We also learn hard lessons about tactics, strategy, fair play, and ethics from dealing with them.

If you don't learn to transcend your hatred of adversaries, you can become controlled by your anger. Before you know it, your loathing turns into paranoia, and your paranoia turns into fear. It is debilitating. While hate may seem to make you more focused and energized in competition, it also makes you less clear thinking, less appealing to friends and would-be allies, and less healthy—mentally, emotionally, physically, and spiritually.

THINK CAREFULLY, WAIT PATIENTLY, ACT BRAVELY

"All that is necessary for the forces of evil to win in the world is for enough good men to do nothing," warned Edmund Burke, the great British statesman. While it may seem prudent to be an innocent bystander while Cain victimizes others, this kind of cowardice and complicity can haunt you for the rest of your life. Be realistic and cautious about when and how you try to isolate or oust Cain, but don't compromise your integrity by letting him get away with wrongdoing.

Remember Mark Twain's advice: "Always do right. This will gratify some people, and astonish the rest."

* * *

One Last Case Study

Since our case studies are meant to be object lessons, they have unhappy endings, much like the original Old Testament story of Cain
and Abel. But who likes an unhappy ending? Even when all of the
evils and afflictions escaped from Pandora's box, mankind was still left
with hope, so let's end with a hopeful story. Perhaps one day soon,
something like this will happen . . . maybe to you.

CASE STUDY 33

Abela and Cainette began work at the same company on the
same day, each taking a job as a "marketing and product manager." They looked alike and dressed alike—power suits and
fashionable glasses—and were jokingly referred to as "the
twins" by their new boss and fellow workers. But Abela and
Cainette couldn't have been more different . . . and it didn't
take long for their colleagues to learn just how different.

Cainette was a schmoozer, especially when playing up to
senior management. She paid close attention to office politics and quickly learned who was friendly with whom, and
who had the power to dispense favors. At first, her staff was

quite taken with her "openness." She was always willing, even eager, to trade gossip about the social and personal lives of others. But her staff was soon shocked to learn that Cainette was using their gossip, which they had considered confidential, as a kind of currency to ingratiate herself with the head of human resources. She was "ratting them out," and they started warning people about how self-serving and even cruel she could be. To Cainette, they were "naive," and she was simply being canny.

Abela had never met anyone like Cainette. She instinctively felt uncomfortable around her and tended to avoid her. Abela couldn't put her finger on just what she distrusted about Cainette until she was given a book by someone Cainette had just fired. The book was called *Cain and Abel at Work*, and when Abela finished reading it, she understood her uneasiness. The demoralized mood in Cainette's department was no accident. It was caused by Cainette's conniving, selfishness, and bad example.

Abela made up her mind to steer clear of Cainette. She politely declined Cainette's invitation to "share concerns" (in writing) about "the lack of direction from senior management." And when Cainette wanted to "pick her brain" about "new marketing strategies" for the company, Abela recognized a trap; Cainette wanted to steal her ideas. Before reading *Cain and Abel at Work*, Abela would have taken these approaches at face value as the casual, even friendly, gestures of a colleague.

Abela concentrated on her work and turned down Cainette's many social invitations to "get together." Abela also took some cautionary steps to protect herself in case Cainette tried to undermine her, as Cainette had already done to several others in the office. Abela went out of her way to keep key people, even those outside of her own department, informed about the progress she and her team were making in serving important clients. She kept detailed records documenting her work on critical projects. And she tried to set a good example for the rest of her team, discouraging gossip and ridicule and encouraging the sharing of credit. Abela never complained about Cainette or anyone else; she was intent on being a problem solver and not becoming a problem herself. Her coworkers, who had first been impressed by Cainette's shrewdness, grew to respect Abela's honest, patient leadership.

Which is why John approached Abela one day and confessed that Cainette had recruited him as a spy, an inside source who was supposed to keep Cainette informed about what was happening in Abela's department. Cainette had also been pressing him for anything he knew about Abela's private life. In return, Cainette had promised him a pay raise ("in the near future") and a promotion ("You'll have your own staff").

Abela knew that there was nothing embarrassing or compromising in her personal life, but she was still understandably upset that Cainette was trying to use people against her by appealing to greed, ego, and the desire for power.

Abela wanted to confront Cainette and tell her off, but recalling advice from *Cain and Abel at Work*, she held back. She remembered how dangerous and devious someone like Cainette could be. Cainette would probably deny everything, and it would come down to one person's word against another. In the meantime, open confrontation would alert Cainette to the fact that Abela was on to her games, and, as the book pointed out, that would make Abela a continuing target for Cainette's intrigue.

Instead, Abela assured John that she would keep their discussion confidential . . . and advised him to do the same. She decided to do the hardest thing imaginable: nothing. Forewarned by John, she at least felt forearmed. She would wait and be ready, confident that in time Cainette would undermine herself and possibly make a fatal mistake.

Over the next few months, Cainette began to sense danger. Several people had complained to upper management about her "constant plotting," and her supervisor had raised the issue with her in a private meeting. Worried about her position, she began looking around for supporters. Seeing that Abela was both well liked and well respected by many people in the company, Cainette set about trying to turn her into an ally. She fawned over Abela with insincere flattery and feigned apologies for past behavior, and she suggested that they "work as a team" on several new projects. Abela politely turned her down. "I'm already stretched too thin," she explained. "I have to focus on doing a good job with the projects I already have on my plate."

When Cainette heard that the company was about to land a major new client, she saw a chance to grab credit and polish her image. A week earlier, she had accidentally run into the prospective client at a cocktail party, where they had made small, meaningless talk for a few minutes. Now, she e-mailed her boss claiming that she had recruited the new client by "pitching him hard" at the cocktail party, a "meeting" she had cleverly engineered precisely for that purpose. She ended her message with "Mission accomplished."

Her boss was excited by the news. After all, since Cainette was a member of his team, her success reflected well on him. He couldn't wait to tell his own boss about Cainette's (and his) coup, and he telephoned his superior immediately. Imagine his surprise when the voice on the other end of the line said, "Hold on a minute. I want you to repeat all this on the speakerphone." When he did, he heard laughter in the background. By coincidence, the new client was sitting in his boss's office at that very moment and was greatly amused to hear that Cainette had "anything to do" with his decision. "It's news to me," the client said.

Humiliated, the boss hung up quickly and called Cainette

. . . onto the carpet. "You made me look like an idiot," he told her. "What's going on here?"

Cainette was desperate, searching in her mind for some way to justify her actions and turn her boss's anger away from herself. "I was wrong, and I'm really, really sorry about it," she said, "but Abela has been taking credit for lots of things she had nothing to do with. Just ask John. He'll back me up." Then she cited several projects for which Abela had supposedly claimed false credit.

It was a serious charge, and Cainette's boss felt he had to look into it. He called John into his office and asked him if Cainette's charges were true.

"No, they're not," John answered. "But Cainette once asked me if I would be willing to say something like this *was* true in order to help her discredit Abela. She promised me Abela's job if Abela was fired, and said she could get me a lot more money. But I'm not going to lie for anyone."

The boss was convinced that John was telling the truth, but he felt it was important to check directly with Abela. Apologetically, he asked her for her side of the story.

Abela barely said a word; she just handed him several documents proving that not only had she been greatly in-volved with the projects in question, but she had also gone out of her way to give her colleagues full credit for their contributions and hard work.

Cainette was fired the next day. "It just hasn't worked out," her boss told her coldly. "And by the way, because of what you told me about Abela, she will also be punished. Her workload will be doubled because she now has to man-age your department as well as hers. Of course, this means that she will also be forced to accept a big salary hike. But she's tough. She can take it."